P9-DNK-144

CRIES FROM THE HALF-WORLD

CRIES from the Half-World

By

FATHER JOHN LEPPICH, S.J.

Original Title
Christus auf der Reeperbahn
Bastion Verlag, Dusseldorf, Germany

Translated by Father Patrick, O.S.B.

SAINT PAUL PUBLICATIONS
Detroit — New York — Canfield — Brookline — Derby

Imprimi Potest:
Rev. Francis X. Borrano, S.S.P.
Provincial Superior

Nihil Obstat:
Rev. Rupert A. Dakoske
Censor Librorum

Imprimatur:
✠ Alexander M. Zaleski, D.D.
Vicar General, Detroit

June 24, 1960

Library of Congress Catalog Card Number: 60-11246

Printed in U. S. A., by Society of St. Paul, New York, N. Y.

PREFACE TO THE ENGLISH EDITION

A church stands poised above a flight of stone steps, and its wrinkled gothic face peers through the early morning shadows into the silence of the city street below, while its spire reaches above the skyline toward God Himself. At this hour there are but two sounds breaking the quiet before the dawn. There is a rattle of bottles as a milkman makes his deliveries and worries about what will happen later in the day when his wife undergoes an operation in the hospital on the other side of town; there is a clatter of heel-plates on concrete as a newsboy jogs off to pick up his papers and wonders if he will sell enough today to supply the amount his widowed mother still needs to make up the rent money.

An old lady, hobbling quietly along the street, is startled by a poor derelict of a man who comes crawling out of the cellar-way which was the only place he had to sleep for the night. The man goes in one direction, and the lady hurries on toward the church to attend early Mass and to pray that her daughter will not drag the family name through the divorce court, but will somehow be reconciled to her husband and patch up their marriage.

The sun rises in the northeast, and the church spire casts a shadow to the southwest. The shadow falls across a pool hall, in the back room of which three men, who have been gambling all night, hold their knives ready to attack and kill a fourth man whom they accuse of cheating.

The sun moves toward the east as it climbs higher in the sky, and the church spire casts a shadow to the west. The shadow falls across a public school as the children are entering, and, once inside, they will be taught reading, writing, arithmetic, history, geography, science—but nothing about religion, God, Christ and His Blessed Mother, sin and virtue, heaven and hell, for all religion, all thought and mention of God is banished from the public schools.

The sun moves to the southeast, going higher into the heavens, and the church spire casts a shadow toward the northwest. The shadow falls across a poor shack of a house in which a mother cries because her children are hungry but there is no food, her babies are cold but there is no coal for the furnace, and the father lies sleeping on the floor, sleeping the sleep brought on by too much strong drink. And the sun and the shadow move on.

The sun is in the west, and the church spire casts a shadow to the east. The shadow falls across a printing plant where the presses are going at top speed, grinding out thousands of copies of immoral books to corrupt the minds and hearts of men, and, in the office, well-dressed executives count up the profits made from the sale of such books.

The sun descends into the northwest, and the church

spire casts a long shadow toward the southeast. The shadow falls across a park where teenage gangs are meeting to plot new adventures into crime and hoodlumism, escapades that will reach the headlines of the newspapers and shock the country.

Finally, the sun sets, and the darkness thickens to hide all manner of evil which will be committed during the night—and it all takes place within the same area over which the church casts its shadow.

Has the Church failed? Has Christianity failed? Not Christianity, but Christians have failed. They have failed because they leave their religion inside the walls of the church building and do not take it with them into their daily lives and into the lives of their fellow men. They go to church and pray their prayers which are as empty as their hearts, and their hearts are empty because they have so little love for God and for their fellow men. Because they pay little attention to anything but their own well-being and comfort, they are unaware of the spiritual and temporal miseries of their brothers. Because they do not heed the cries from the half-world of sin born of poverty and suffering, they stand as it were before God, like Cain when he had murdered his brother, and they say by their lives, more eloquently than with words: "Am I my brother's keeper?"

These are some of the considerations that moved Father Leppich to write CHRISTUS AUF DER REEPERBAHN, basing his remarks on actual experience in bringing solace to the unfortunate.

And so, my dear reader, turn the pages and peruse

the contents of this book, but as you do so, be prepared to have the author open your heart, while the poor and the miserable and the spiritually bankrupt cry out from the half-world, and pluck with persistent fingers at your heartstrings.

– The Editor

CONTENTS

CHRIST
on the Reeperbahn

O LORD, the Reeperbahn is a sad advertisement for Hamburg. But may we dare to put on the prophet's mantle, and with the threatening voice of Jeremias, brand Your big city as a daughter of Sodom?

And why?

The Reeperbahn is everywhere.

It is in the Bowery in New York.

It is in Montmartre in Paris.

It is in the harbor section of Hongkong.

And it is in many a small town and village—in the neighborhood of Your Church.

Of this we speak in this book.

O Lord, let it not become something cheap and hackneyed!

We wish above all to erect Your Cross in those places which man, with weary resignation, has left to the devil —the places of entertainment, the variety shows, the stadium, the dance hall, the big-business world, the world of nylon, neon lights, and plexiglass.

For since You sat at table with publicans and sinners (it was held against You), Your disciples are also called into this half-world.

And no one of us has the right to condemn such haunts of evil.

Woe, if the Christian religion has become so anemic that it can no longer heal the sinful world!

Woe if one makes a misstep on the tightrope!

Much has been written about this half-world. But only a few dare to make the religious diagnosis and then pronounce the helping word. For Your "Ego te absolvo" should be spoken there also, and especially there.

And then, Lord, those in authority do not wish to admit that the masses go in and out of the bedlam of sin—the masses of whom you said again and again: "I have pity on the crowd."

For they also should drink of pure water; they should not be left to satisfy their thirst out of puddles and swamps, nor to wash down the last remains of their self-control with alcohol.

But, Lord, what good does it do to lament?

Should not the fact that You Yourself dwell in the most evil district of Hamburg at 43 Great Freedom Street, make us sit up and take notice?

Is it really so difficult to talk about virtue in this moral jungle?

Do not men live there also whose feet tread the streets of the big city, but whose heads rest in heaven? Are there not many upright men in these big cities who see, and yet do not see, the cheap attractions which the devil proffers from his repertoire?

Does the world really consist of gangsters and thugs?

Are there not among them some who are led astray, fallen and stranded, yet who, in their inner being long for righteousness? If only You would reach out to them!

Yes, Lord, Satan knows them—the taverns and the bars, the dancers and the taxi girls. But You also know them and You know them better. And You love them.

Therefore, You seek them out. You made no exception in the mission You gave us for these, Your endangered children in the devil's carnival, even if their sins gleam in all colors of the rainbow. But do not let Your disciples lack courage in this daring mission.

It is a consoling thought that Your holy sanctuary lamp burns unceasingly in the churches, and at the very same time that the bright lights of the night-clubs flash. And while sinners indulge their evil desires in the night, Your monks are awakened from sleep during the same hours to make reparation by prayer in choir. This is what this book is about.

O Lord, accompany us with Your blessing, while we are spreading your message.

CHRIST
and the Sinner

LORD and Master, the police have records in which certain people are listed as criminals, vagrants, and prostitutes. The world scorns them, but You are concerned with them because of their immortal souls, and You keep an eternal record of them. Indeed, they have daily and constantly degraded their bodies, the temples of the Holy Spirit, and have justly deserved Your punishment and scorn. But when I read Your Holy Scripture, I am greatly consoled because You in Your mercy spoke the most beautiful words about them—words in which Your goodness and Your love shine forth.

With what tenderness You met the holy Magdalen who, like them, was once a street walker. Perhaps you knew it much better than those Pharisees, who were responsible for this woman's shame and, nevertheless condemned her bitterly. How many abused and persecuted women have, through reckless emotion, sunk into this abyss? Not to speak of the many who, made desperate by their children's needs and hunger, have been reduced to this evil means of supporting them.

It is indeed true that in every woman there is a sinner and a saint. But how many have strayed into the way of sin? No one cares enough for their souls to show them the way back. One cannot help them with vice raids, hygienic precautions, or police protection. Only You, good Master, can save them, when You meet them as You met Magdalen. And they will thank You with fidelity and gratitude like that which Magdalen showed when she followed You even to the cross.

And you, O Mother Mary, help us to remember that these despised women are also under your mantle.

CHRIST
on the Boulevards of Paris

IN Notre Dame, the Cathedral of Paris, during the Easter liturgy, a young student in a stolen Dominican habit ascended the pulpit of the overcrowded Cathedral and shouted: *"God is dead!"*

The worshipers were disturbed and astounded. Police came, arrested the man, and took him to an asylum.

But why did they arrest this young man? Is one crazy when today, in the twentieth century, he speaks out what the sparrows whistle from the roofs?

You are right, young student. Ask your comrades who study in Paris at the Sorbonne, powerhouse of the intellectual hierarchy. Here in a European atmosphere—nay more, a cosmopolitan atmosphere—the great leaders of Asian politics have studied. In this same atmosphere, while I was once in the lecture hall of the faculty of medicine, I had the following experience: The student near me handed me his notebook because he noticed that, being a foreigner, I could not follow the professor. I asked this understanding Frenchman about Paris and about his studies, and then, discreetly, I inquired about his attitude towards his religion.

This young student was well educated. He was too well educated not to be interested in religious questions. But he was no more interested in Christ than in a statue of Buddha, which he would esteem for its antiquarian value. Among the educated there is tolerance, but for this man Christ is a God without life.

To change the awkward subject, he handed me a cigarette. God was dead for him. So the heretic in Notre Dame was right. But, I thought, in the simple people Christ still lives; in them He is not yet dead. To the ragged figures who live under the bridges of the Seine, God is still near. These slum dwellers who warm themselves in the winter on the gratings of the subway, they at least must have a more intimate knowledge of their poor Brother, Christ. Among these poor I hoped that I should still find God. They did not recognize me as a priest. There are so many strange people on the Champs-Elysees that a foreign priest makes no impression.

But for these outcasts also God was dead.

Perhaps He was smothered in rubbish, drowned in whiskey. Perhaps eaten by vermin, frozen or starved under the bridges. No! I realized that these outcasts looked upon God as a luxury reserved for the wealthy.

Perhaps the girl on the street corner still knows God? She has a sinful sister, named Magdalen, who longed for Christ. And Christ did indeed seek out the sinners. When she came up and spoke to me, I sent her away with a brusque: NO! Was that right? Should I not have reproached her openly for her wrongdoing? Should I not have spoken of God? I believed so—and hurried after her. I no longer know what I said to her—I spoke of her unworthy life, of sin, of the good Samaritan. She only patted me on the shoulder and said, "You are a fool." So I am mad. For her also God is dead.

I no longer had courage to speak to others. I was as one of the disciples on the way to Emmaus, going home disconsolate and despairing, to whom all seemed lost. Thus it is with God in Paris. God is dead. Yes, I admit it. I had no more courage to speak about God. Even Josephine, the maid in the hotel, looked at me strangely when I again approached the subject. And Fernand, also, the blind salesman on the street, did not take me seriously; nor did the ragged old man in front of the museum, who offers his matches with a hoarse: "Allumettes, allumettes!"

Christ is dead?

The young heretic in Notre Dame was right. God is dead. He is dead in the night clubs and in the bars. He is dead in the offices and in the factories. He is dead even among the poor and the beggars whom He loved so much.

Why then did they arrest the student?

One is a fool, Lord Jesus Christ, to mention Your name on the streets of Paris. Indeed, Notre Dame Cathedral stands there. But it is considered as a museum piece, and the priests inside are thought of as museum caretakers. Have You cursed the city as You did Jerusalem? I have not met any saints there who still honor Your name. Or am I too weak and faithless? For You can sow seed on the asphalt of Paris and give it growth. In this stone desert of the big city, Your children are dying of the thirst for religion. But You can draw water out of the rocks. Do that, Lord, also in Paris. This Paris is everywhere in the world!

CHRIST
on the Billboards

O LORD, I hate these billboards which have become a brothel of advertising. I hate these placarded walls and the men who inspire them. Such men care for nothing but selling their goods; selfishly, cynically and crudely, they deceive the common people. They are full of lies. They embrace, as with the arms of an octopus, the poorest of our people who blandly trust in their recommendations.

I hate the voice of the loud-speakers that shout at me on the streets. I am powerless as they beat against my undeserving ears.

I hate these radios that persecute me even to the remotest corner and rob me of rest.

I hate the modern automobiles that promise me the solitude of nature, but continually deafen me with radio music.

I hate the harvest fairs and the agricultural fairs which throw together an artificial paradise out of paste and plaster and plywood.

The billboards entice and charm and coax; they have become the cover girl of business; they do not aim to satisfy needs but to create them.

I hate these advertisements, against which I can no longer fight. On thousands of subway steps in Paris, again and again, I read in big bright letters the word Dubonnet, Dubonnet, Dubonnet. I do not know what it is, but now I believe in Dubonnet, like the other millions who must read the word over and over.

And if tomorrow the advertising agent of the devil should write a thousand times "God is dead!" I believe it would not be easy, in the face of such propaganda, to be convinced of the opposite.

Yes, Lord, I hate this advertising of the devil's wares on billboards, in radio programs, and in catalogues. And yet, Lord, all the curses in the Old Testament do not help me. In the advertising storm of Satan the man of today has lost his antenna for God.

But we cannot permit the highways and byways to become Satan's playground. The children of this world should not be wiser than we. Give us Your Holy Spirit so that, when the opportunity arrives, we may bring your message to the deluded people of today.

CHRIST
in the Circus

IT is a strange thing. Missionaries go to the African fire-eater and to the Eskimos, to the Indians of America and of Asia, and five thousand miles is not too far for them to go. But outside the small city—not ten minutes away—there is a circus with Indians from America and from Asia, and no missionary goes there. We pass by these circus people in their homes as though they were still outlawed, like the vulgar minstrels, charlatans, and vagabonds of the Middle Ages.

Priests bless the plow horses of the farmers; they have a blessing even for the pigs in the stall—and that is good. But why do they not also bless the lions in the circus that threaten their trainers, the horses that bear the riders? Priests bless the tractor; why do they not also bless the trapeze and the rope on which the performers risk their lives for the entertainment of their fellow men?

One day I went to the circus city. Perhaps I would not have had the courage to do so if the group of dancers and trapeze artists had not invited me. There in the circus, accompanied by the roaring of lions, I gave my first talk to the circus people.

I learned to know them. And I must apologize to these circus folk; I had not known that the entertainment they offered was so clean and wholesome. I had not known that, because of their work, the young dancers live a strict, ascetic life, and in the evening go down on their knees to pray. I had not known that, because no pastor takes care of them, the merry, laughing clown, with touching fatherly care, teaches his children religion in the wagon which is their home.

I had not known that two Chinese children longed for baptism, and no one gave it to them; that the tightrope walker made the sign of the cross before every performance, so that God would help him to give real joy by his act.

Nowadays there is a special chaplain for the circus, and the people behind the colorful curtains are proud of their pastor. He is well liked, and his flock is glad to see him. A certain circus director even provides him with a plane ticket so that he can take care of the spiritual needs of a circus in Scandinavia.

One day, after the blessing of the animals, a well-known circus rider came to the priest and said: "Father, I was not present for the blessing of the animals. But now I do not dare to mount my horse because I feel unsafe; come, please, and bless *my* horse too!"

Superstition? Who will decide where the sacramentals, for some people, edge over into magic and superstition? How often is superstition found among our best Christians? At any rate, Christ is present wherever the very least faith is to be found. And we should imitate Christ in this respect.

The circus chaplain faces new tasks. He becomes chaplain of the show people. He writes in the newspapers about these people, about their careers and their responsibilities. His opinions carry weight. After a good program he interviews the star who, five minutes before, had been loudly applauded. "My dear young lady, your number is good. But why did you tell that joke with a double meaning?"

"Father, no one has ever before suggested that it is wrong to tell such jokes. Thank you for telling me."

Does it then depend on us? Why have we never told these people that they sometimes make a mistake? Perhaps they have been waiting for such criticism from priests or laymen. For variety shows and circuses are not a spiritual no-man's land, nor a terrain of the devil. Let us not forget this.

Above, in the audience, sit masses of men who no longer attend our churches. If we do not go to the circus to preach to the spectators, we can at least speak to the performers and artists who entertain with their program. This program can bring genuine, wholesome delight to the spellbound audience, and it can be a Christian work. But if we make no attempt to reach these people, thousands may lose their souls. We do not reckon that such efforts will be a hundred percent successful. But if we do nothing, we have no room for complaint.

Shall these crowds of men really be lost to God? There is reason to fear this because once it was so—at the time when the crowd shouted its hosannas to the divine Caesars in the Circus Maximus, and with its cries of "crucify" caused the Christians to be thrown to the beasts in the arena.

Christ in the circus! Here we have missed an important task.

"O Lord," a saint has said, "He has spent his life best who has brought joy to the greatest number of men." Grant that the performers and circus riders may bring genuine joy—joy that is not spotted and tarnished by the poisonous smoke of the devil. Let them feel that they too are serving God, if they begin their work with the Sign of the Cross. And grant that the many millions of men who go to the circus may feel something of the genuine joy of the children of God.

CHRIST
and the Dancer

"A favorable day came when Herod on his birthday gave a banquet to the officials, tribunes, and chief men of Galilee. And Herodias' own daughter having come in and danced, pleased Herod and his guests. And the king said to the girl, 'Ask of me what thou willest, and I will give it to thee.' And he swore to her, 'Whatever thou dost ask, I will give thee, even though it be the half of my kingdom.' And she went out and said to her mother, 'What am I to ask for.' And she said, 'The head of John the Baptist.' And she came in at once with haste to the king, and asked, saying, 'I want thee right away to give me on a dish the head of John the Baptist.' And, grieved as he was, the king, because of his oath and his guests, was unwilling to displease her. But sending an executioner, he commanded that his head be brought on a dish. Then he beheaded him in the prison, and brought his head on a dish, and gave it to the girl; and the girl gave it to her mother."

This is not an excerpt from a script for a Hollywood horror film. No, what you have just read is from the sixth chapter of the Gospel according to St. Mark.

Salome–she is the prototype of the loose women in the international cabarets, as well as those who, with pretended modesty, ensnare men by a carefully concealed lust and make them murder their souls.

Herod–he is the prototype of the influential playboys who squander their possessions at the gaming tables and hide their own evil lives under the cloak of "tolerance" and "liberal" morality.

Herodias–she is the prototype of those unnatural mothers who dress their half-grown daughters in a "sexy" fashion, to catch the eye of possible husbands. And she is also the prototype of those modern mothers who, with their "liberal" standards, allow their children an almost criminal freedom, and thus, in their blind ape-love, murder the souls of their children.

CHRIST
and Television

SATURDAY, 10:30 P.M. First act of the play. The television studio: a confusion of contraptions and spotlights. On the stool, the announcer, a made-up beauty wearing heavy cosmetics, who, with suitable smiles, awaits the light signal to announce the program. She has many wares to offer, among the others, *God.*

On the other side, a priest, who—what irony—likewise is made-up and, between men with black glasses, awaits the red light.

Second act of the play.

Bar in St. Pauli. The bartender understands his work and mixes his cocktails with ritual solemnity.

Girls employ their most seductive voices to entice a few soldiers, and to induce them to buy the most expensive drinks as often as possible.

Half asleep, and inwardly bored by their partners, to whom they give sweet, artificial smiles, they watch the television that is showing a movie in the semi-darkness of the bar.

Then the announcement: "Now follows a word for Sunday."

"Honey, turn the set off! A priest is going to talk." But the priest has already begun. Is it curiosity? Or secret interest? Whatever it may be, they listen. A full eight minutes . . . here and in many thousands of rooms, cafes, and homes.

"Ladies and gentlemen! I consider it dangerous to put on a religious program at this hour. The Gospel is not sleeping powder, but dynamite. And that is dangerous for you at so late an hour.

"Take a look at the clock, please. Now, in these eight minutes, about eight thousand men will die. Others lie on operating tables somewhere, without hope, under anesthetics. During these eight minutes, on the banks of the Seine in Paris, or elsewhere, despairing women stand in the last seconds before their suicide. In damp prison cellars men are tortured so that a confession may be forced from them.

"This is all happening during these eight minutes while we are in the chair before the television screen, while we let the Sunday bells, as background music, sentimentally twinkle in our ears.

"But what does that mean to you? Do you think this is an affair for the state, or for the police, or for the welfare agencies? If you think so, you are no Christian, but you are a spiritual brother of the murderer, Cain. He also asked: 'Am I my brother's keeper?'

"You ask what you can do?

"Is it difficult to know that? You should help your brothers, the sick, the dying, and the hungry, the imprisoned.

"How can you do that?

"Look, I will not tear open your purse now, but your heart.

"Let us take an example.

"We have modern hospitals with all modern comforts; they are as soulless as factories with mass production. And we have sick rooms that are desolate. In these, the souls of the sick must freeze. You can help your sick brother by means of a letter, by a visit, by a book, by an alms. Have you ever thought of that?

"And our men in prison!

"I do not mean only the men in our local prisons. I mean prisoners of all kinds—including our men who are still held captive in Russia. We should help them with our prayers.

"And those in our penal institutions. I have met young first offenders in prison, who, without God, have become delinquents because their mothers did not teach them to pray. Come, we wish to be good to them. They need our help. Listen, we seek big brothers, big sisters, who are ready to do a service for their fellowmen who are in prison. Even if they do nothing but pray for the success of the difficult work of the prison chaplain!

"And then, the drunkards!

"In one big city of Germany there are five thousand alcoholics. That means that five thousand mothers are weeping for their sons; five thousand wives are crushed; thousands of children despise their fathers. Your fellow worker who is an alcoholic is still a Christian and your brother. Say a word to him. Take him by the arm on pay day and lead him home. We need five thousand guardian angels on the sidewalks of this big city alone. Let not this brotherly favor to the alcoholics be undone.

"And our orphans!

"Every fifth child in Germany must do without a father or mother because one of them has broken his marriage vows. And because of that the child is punished and hurt. It hungers for love. A plant in the cellar without light becomes pale and yellow. A child without love pines away and may become a delinquent. Do not say that you cannot help. We are waiting for the bricks to build our family orphanages. Your dog, perhaps, sleeps on a wool blanket, and our little ones beg you for this blanket.

"Yes, we sit comfortably before the television set and prepare for Sunday—a Sunday on which we can rest, on which our table is richly spread. But do not forget that millions will not have a piece of bread. We are overfed, but thousands of children in Asia look despairingly to their mothers, who cannot set anything before them. If you would at least give us the price of the bread that you and your children throw away, perhaps with it we could save a life. If each of your children could give just a package of dried milk, we could perhaps save hundreds from starvation.

"Do you see now that the gospel of love of neighbor can be dynamite?

"And now, at the end of this telecast shall I say: 'Gracious lady, I wish you a restful night?'

"No, if you have done nothing, if you as a Christian

do not wish to help, then I wish you a *restless* night. For, do not forget, you stretch out in a fresh bed, while hundreds and thousands of innocents die in dirt and stench. While we sleep peacefully, there are thousands who freeze and starve, weep and shiver.

"We dare not lie sleeping like the cattle, but we should feel conscience in us like a thorn. We should know that we are all brothers, brothers who have been redeemed with the same Blood of Jesus Christ. And we are also brothers who will face one another in eternity. Then we shall see our last television.

"And the program? No industrial fair, no film festival, no horse race with accompanying fashion show, no beautiful ladies nor bar frequenters, no, but a truly horrifying program. And then you will not be able to turn off the set. It will be a program with the latest developments in technicolor, in which you will see children with eyes yellowed by malaria. It will be television combined for the first time with odors; you will smell the stench and rottenness of lepers, who will look at you reproachfully.

"And by way of sensation, it will be a telecast in which the starved Chinese coolies, frozen blue with cold, will step bodily out of the screen and will accuse you and call you to a reckoning before God. These are the ones about whom you will maintain that you knew nothing.

"Now you may turn off your television. Eight minutes have passed. But please do not turn away your hearts. Help. There is still time!

"You can no longer open the eyes of the dead in those mass graves. But you can help to bring light to the living who are almost overcome by suffering.

"If you wish to do that—but only then—I wish you a restful and blessed night."

CHRIST
and the Passivists

IN Russia, it is the greatest insult to call a man a "passivist." But long before Bolshevism, Christ castigated the behavior of the passivists. You must again take up Holy Scripture. It is no soothing, edifying reading for the evening. If you read it correctly, you can no longer fall peacefully asleep. Have you read the passage in the Holy Gospel according to St. Mark, Chapter 11, verses 11 to 14?

Christ curses the barren fig tree, which immediately dries up to the very roots. Thus Christ curses the lukewarm, the passive, and the indifferent among us. And the words of the Apocalypse sound like the rumbling of a storm threatening the Church.

"I would that thou wert cold or hot. But because thou art lukewarm, and neither cold nor hot, I am about to vomit thee out of my mouth."

So often we satisfy ourselves with our "should," and we sleep at our posts, while we should be active if we expect a reward in eternity. Do we know at all how great, measured by our talents, our "should" is?

O Lord, you are right in pronouncing Your curse

on the slacker. Because we have buried our talents and because, by reason of our love of comfort and laziness, Satan has gained ground. Because by too much "tolerance" we have lost our religious backbone. Because we have feared that, by taking action, we should be accused of fanaticism, and have not had the courage to be a fool for Jesus Christ. Because we have spent our Christian life listlessly, and we have led no man to You. Because we have supported the reporter of Satan by buying bad newspapers. Because we have not turned away from poisoned radio broadcasts and pornographic films. Because we have not cried out against the sins of social injustice. Because our hearts are like ice-boxes, they reject our brothers who suffer need. Because we contribute a few pennies, whereas even the Jews gave a tenth of their goods. Because of all these things, Satan has gained ground.

Yes, Lord and Master, You forgave a murderer and took him to Yourself, because he repented at the end of his life. But You will curse us if we have not brought forth the fruit that you expect from us. The thought of the cursed and dried-up fig tree falls like an evil omen on our idleness. Has not this idleness already become the repose of a cemetery where our idealism lies buried?

But no, Lord, we wish to take Your word seriously so that this curse may not come upon us for eternity.

CHRIST
and the Super-activists

TWO ministers met. One of them complained: "I do everything for my community. I erected the church; I had a club room built; I am present at all the social affairs; I organize excursions; every week there is a dance; I have founded a sports club. I provide first class talent for our regular church concerts—but it is all useless. I cannot get the people into the church."

The other answered: "How would it be if you gave religion a trial?"

One might smile at this as a good joke if it did not express bitter irony and tragedy at the same time.

A man may mean well when he presides over seven societies and cooperates with five others, sings in the church choir and keeps busy with charitable works—until one day he notices that he has exhausted his energy and in body and soul can do no more.

There are such super-activists also in the purely worldly sphere, whose feverish activity keeps themselves and others out of breath. In the political arena it often happens among the best Christians that the wife becomes a political widow. We do not wish to speak here of the well-known business tycoons.

This picture, however, is saddest in the religious field, especially when the super-activist wears a cassock, when he represents the heretical thesis: "One must neglect God for the sake of men and for love," and when he has "no time to become a saint" (and yet, that is our principal task). He is then so far gone that he considers a real inner religious life a luxury.

One cannot build the kingdom of God on the ruins of one's own spiritual life.

He who has been in the solitude of the desert can give nothing to men. He remains a ship of shallow draft and can at most be set in shallow waters. He who does not daily wrestle with God will not be able to teach his searching brothers. For one cannot religiously flirt with God; it is necessary to wrestle with Him as Jacob did with the angel.

Furthermore there is the well-known Catholic demagogue who, on the platform of a Catholic society, shows off his natural abilities. He becomes a routine religious functionary, who tomorrow can be active in another direction. But he soon disillusions his hearers.

In the care of souls grace cannot be replaced with psychology and charm, neither among priests nor among the laity.

You will find a classical answer in the Gospel according to St. Luke. (10:30-42) Even one who is not much at home in Holy Scripture knows of the event which took place when Christ visited His friend Lazarus, and his sisters, Mary and Martha.

Martha had no time to devote to the guest because

she was so busy in the house and in the kitchen trying to offer the best to their guest. She is over-active in external things and has no understanding of the spiritual longings of her sister. She took offense at Mary, who did nothing but sit at the feet of the Master and listen to Him. Then Christ spoke the well-known words: "Martha, Martha, thou art anxious and troubled about many things; and yet only one thing is needful. Mary has chosen the best part, and it will not be taken away from her."

In the kingdom of God we need active persons who can work, plan, and organize untiringly for God. But they remain like a motor idling, and they become unsympathetic troublemakers in their own sphere if they do not keep their antenna continually turned towards God. That is, they must not rely solely on their own capabilities, but must also pray. Without prayer no prophet has announced his message. Christ always withdrew into solitude to pray.

Lord Jesus Christ, great is the number of those activists whom we have gathered into Your service. You know their zeal and their devotion. But do not let us become mere "super-activists" who forget the royal task of prayer. And let us remain true to our resolution to accomplish the holy exercises as the foundation to our fidelity. For such days of recollection make converts to sanctity.

CHRIST
and the Cardinal

BY this I do not mean the American best-seller, that book which is a sensation among even non-denominational readers. I am thinking of another cardinal, one whose tragedy reminds us of the man whom Christ designated as "the greatest one born of woman." You must read this passage yourself in the Gospel according to St. Matthew. (11:1-115)

This John became the sensation of Judea. All came to him: foreign legionaries and ladies of the elite of Jerusalem, rich vineyard owners and rough harbor workers. And John does not make it easy for them! His sermon is not for the perfumed ears of the high society; his words often flay like scourges and whips. For he had been called to make straight the way of the Messias, and he has the honorable title of "forerunner of Christ." So much did he deny himself in the service of the Lord.

One is inclined to believe that Christ, out of gratitude, would protect him with His miraculous power from all evil and injustice. Certainly, trouble soon followed in the wake of this uncomfortable preacher of penance.

On account of an adulteress he was thrown into prison and—there forgotten. Outside, in the streets of Palestine, hosannas were shouted for Him for Whom John had worked, and Who, at that same time, was inquiring about John. That was John's darkest hour. We do not know whether or not he threatened to forsake Christ when he sent the two messengers to Him.

Today, hardly a thousand miles away, there sits a Hungarian Cardinal, likewise a prisoner. He has worn himself out in the service of the Lord. And now he is forgotten. Perhaps he hears the bells of the distant cathedral. Does no one think of him?

Perhaps he hears of the luxury-busses that go to Rome on pilgrimages; he hears of splendid Katholiken-Tagen and great congresses of Christian people, who, judging by the hosannas, will have nothing to do with the "crucify" of the Hungarian persecutors.

Perhaps that is the greatest John-like tragedy and the most difficult burden on the faith of these men. And the tragedy becomes cynical in big European cities where fake Patriarchs are led around like parade-horses as a sign of religious tolerance; and some Christian churchmen deal peacefully with these Russian "state bishops" while cardinals languish in prison.

Pardon me! Must I correct myself?

The Soviet regime, "friendly to the Church," let one cardinal go free. Who? A cardinal who in the flower of his manhood could stand before his people in the office of prophet? No, a shadow, a broken man, who was released from prison only to be confined in a private house, whereabouts unknown; a cardinal who had been diabolically robbed of his understanding with drugs. For this is what Satan whispered into the ears of the bolshevistic people's court. The mock trial and the martyrdom of a Stephen would, at that time, have been a splendid testimony for the teaching of Jesus Christ—in order to prevent that, the successors of Stephen must be brainwashed before the mock trial begins.

St. John became a martyr. This is one of the most honorable titles in the Church. But Satan and the members of his party need no more martyrs in their program.

The joy over the cardinal's release was premature. His name has now sunk into oblivion like the murdered freedom of Hungary.

The torture of the cardinal in Hungary continues, and he is apparently forgotten.

But woe to the Freemasons of the West; woe to the reporters of Satan, who write whole books about the divorce of an actress, but ignore the martyrdom of this hero!

Christ has not forgotten this cardinal. He has always been with him, in his prison cell as well as at his mock trial.

But is Christ still with us in the West? One could have his doubts about this in our sated West, which is steeped in humanitarian activities, while it passes over great crimes against mankind "on dogmatic grounds."

Do not believe that you have done something when

you allow yourself to be chloroformed by your own sympathy in a single demonstration of protest. If the suffering of the cardinal is not brought to our minds again and again, Christianity in the West is a mere facade.

We know, O Lord, from Your Holy Scripture, that the ancient Church prayed without ceasing for St. Peter when he was in prison. But Your servants and Your witnesses today are still held in prisons. Hundreds of bishops and priests are tortured by the hangmen of Satan.

Full of admiration, we have given to Your confessors the honorable title of the "Silent Church," and that is in accord with truth. But woe to us who could have spoken, but who, for the sake of comfort, have become the silent and *sleeping* Church!

Through our prayers and sacrifices we wish to stand by our persecuted brothers so that we may wake up before the trumpets sound at the last judgment.

CHRIST
and Europe

THERE are experiences that shock one to the marrow. In a London suburb I met a Negro who was studying for his doctorate at the university. He was a man of much experience and knew the whole world.

I questioned him: "What do you think of Europe?" He became very serious and said: "Europe is going down; it has murdered God."

I cannot forget that statement. Must a Negro say that to us? Do you think he was wrong? Then let us throw a spotlight on old Europe.

Europe—that means England! How Christianity must have become mere carpets and drapery when Ghandi, a pagan, who, however, still believed in God, could shake the whole Christian commonwealth! In Henry VIII, an adulterer sat on the throne—an adulterer who led astray a whole country with its glorious Christian tradition of the Church—a country where, in general, cathedrals are now nothing but museums.

Europe—that means Sweden! There the standards of living is higher than in any other country of Europe. It is known that the number of children there is the lowest in all Europe. In such prosperity God is suffocated.

Europe—that means Poland, where a social, progressive, and political Catholicism, stamped by Moscow, causes chaos and division, and the Red Party Book has replaced the Bible.

Europe—that means Austria, where there are often three abortions for one birth, to call down God's judgment!

Europe—that means France, the great nation! There God was murdered by the harlot whom the Revolution placed on the altar of Notre Dame.

Europe—the countries of the Balkans, where Christ daily and hourly is trodden on and persecuted in the persons of hundreds of priests and nuns.

Europe—that means Germany, for centuries the religiously split and bleeding heart of the continent—the nation of philosophers who erected the first chair of atheism.

Europe—there are also the countries of Italy and Spain that are still Catholic as a whole. But we worry and fear about the capability of these bulwarks of the true faith to hold out against communism.

Europe—that was once the western land bringing the peoples of the earth to God.

Europe—that is not only a political or geographic idea—it is you, it is I, it is all of us!

We need not be the worst pessimists to affirm that Europe is on the decline. For it has murdered God. Not as the Jews did; they still reckoned with Christ—but *we* ignore Him!

We have no right to condemn Russia with its state

atheism. Among us there is in millions of hearts and heads private atheism, which is far more dangerous and destructive.

Perhaps we are too "tolerant" to deny God, but we wound Him and kill Him with silence. We have imprisoned Him in the cathedral and preserved Him in the museum. We have made Him a dainty toy for a few sentimental Christmas days, which, after the feast, is packed away again in cotton.

Have we not murdered God?

Not in atheistic conferences, but in our life; in our families where the cross over the marriage bed has become a lie; in every unborn child, killed by an unmortified mother; in schools that feed our children with pap, and that have made religion an elective course for backward, pious people; in our parliaments, from which some would like to remove all Christian principles; in many of our Marxist businesses which are scrupulously free from all religion, and where, among business men, only dividends count, and not the welfare of the workers; in the officials of our state, who constantly marry and divorce; in our universities, where atheism is openly injected into the young listeners; in our neutral newspapers, which place religion alongside the sport and stock news, and that only because one must have consideration for the Christian readers; in illustrated magazines where reporters of Satan jump like vultures on scandals and sensational tales about marriage, and murder God in the souls of the young.

And we remain silent!

We all murder God if we remain silent when we should speak. For whoever is not for God is against Him. In regard to God there is no neutrality. And so all nihilists and lukewarm persons become foreign legionaries of Satan, because those who no longer pray are already practical atheists.

If you say: "True, I do not pray any more, but I am not an atheist," then I can only answer: "Woe to you: the brother-murderer, Cain, and the betrayer of Christ also do not pray any more. Hence you find yourself in their company." When that happens to just one person it is tragic enough. But woe when it happens to a whole people! The end is spiritual bankruptcy. All Europe seems to be near to that.

Who will save it?

Not Karl Marx, with his communistic pipe dream. And certainly not the substitute religion of capitalistic big business. Nor the Freemasons with their worldly ideals.

Only the Cross of Christ can still save Europe and give us spiritual security and an answer to life.

Lord, the truth always hurts, especially when a pagan like this Negro throws it into our faces within sight of our cathedral. But You forgave the city of Nineve when it changed its ways. Let our bells in the towers become storm bells that this Europe may listen once more and find its way back to You before You inflict Your punishment on the West.

CHRIST
and the 293 Sects

IT was no empty speculation when in the famous Hyde Park in London, on the podium of the "Catholic Evidence Guild," I gave my religious lecture alongside the preachers of the sects. My broken English awakened sympathy among the English (who at any rate are too polite to laugh at the stuttering of a foreigner). They must have felt something like interest in the stranger who tortured himself with their language. At any rate, they listened.

This speakers' corner in Hyde Park is interesting. Under the open heaven dozens of preachers of different sects give their talks. The listeners go from one to another, and the speaker who speaks most fervently or stirs up the most lively discussion has the largest audience. Normally these are the fervent communists and the Catholics.

This fact is surprising and at the same time tragic. Is that the one teaching of Jesus Christ that offers itself in numberless sects? Where is its unity if it can split into 293 sects? (Who knows their real number? This estimate is certainly too low.) Among these are sects which cancel each other out with the same message. How could things come to such a pass?

The reformation in Germany caused the split with the greatest result. It might have meant well in the beginning. But it unchained a Hydra, like that fabulous snake that grew two new heads for every one that was cut off.

The more man makes himself the measure of all things and prefers to attain his happiness according to his own plan, the more dangerous grows the religious indifference which rules millions today. "It does not matter what one believes as long as one lives an upright life," "all religions are alike," "we all believe in the same God": these are the sayings which lead to the worship of false gods.

This vague big-heartedness is tantamount to religious suicide. At any rate, Christ did not give us this freedom when he said: "He who does not believe will be condemned."

Along with this religious indifference, religious subjectivism and comfort lead to the forming of sects. Every chatterbox and enthusiast thinks he can interpret Holy Scripture according to his own sentimental opinions. He picks out individual truths and cloaks them in enthusiastic mysticism. And then, home-made truths are sold like ballons from a stick. But he overlooks one thing. Protestant scholars have discovered three thousand imperfections in the translation of Luther.

Without doubt the sects have great success today. It may be that the cold hearts of some Christians have driven many of our inquiring confreres into the arms of the active sects. Thousands of men go to them in the uncertainty of war time and in the post-war period, having lost their normal judgment. They also attract many men who are mentally lazy and uncritical.

The fact is that those who belong to sects acquire a burning belief in their sect that can only put us Christians to shame. It is hardly necessary to speak of the near-maniacal conviction of the "earnest bible students" with their fanatical hatred of the Church and their feeble efforts to interpret the Bible.

To be taken more seriously are other Protestant sects, like the Quakers and the Salvation Army, who, after the Catholic Church, form the greatest social power of the present day, although they often seem to replace care of the soul with care of the body.

Besides, there is a flood of theosophic societies, who embellish their new Indian-pantheistic teaching with Christian thought, and mix occultism, Freemasonry, philosophy and religion with one another. They have won numerous followers because the exotic and mystical have a special charm today.

But we dare not be satisfied with consideration of the history of religions. Every genuine Catholic weeps for a church that bleeds from a thousand wounds.

Holy Mother Church at all times protects Holy Scripture as a precious inheritance, and holds fast to the Epistle to the Galatians: "But even if we or an angel from heaven should preach a gospel to you other than that which we have preached to you, let him be anathema.'" (Gal., 1:8) Whoever changes even an iota has already corrupted the teaching of Christ. But the editions of the Bible put out by the sects have been changed, shortened, enlarged, and hence falsified.

Besides, for them the Bible is the only source of revelation. But this single source can become a book of heresy because, as St. Peter says, it is difficult to understand. Without doubt, there is need of a teaching authority to protect our religion and to keep it pure; otherwise all the truth of faith will be lost in the flood. And this teaching office has been entrusted to the one Holy Catholic and Apostolic Church, to which the Holy Ghost has been promised until the end of time. In the religious Babylon and impenetrable darkness of today, it stands like a lighthouse.

The Church has never declared Holy Scripture to be a sole, magic means of salvation, but has always called on infallible tradition. This tradition tells us that Christianity was blossoming at a time when the New Testament had not as yet been written.

How could the Bible be our only guide, when the printing press was not invented until the fifteenth century, before which time it was impossible to produce a large number of copies! Therefore, the expensive and hand-written copies were chained, like the telephone book today, so that they could not be stolen. Nevertheless, Catholics had already published fourteen complete editions when Luther, in 1522, put out his first Bible.

A much greater thorn in the eye of the attackers is the One True Church. What gives her the right to such "arrogance" and "intolerance?" The faith she teaches is the same for all; it is one and indivisible. There is in our Church no hidden teaching for the privileged. The same doctrine of Jesus Christ is for the pope and for the workingman.

Hence one cannot split off a partial truth, a section (from which we derive the word "sect") without endangering the edifice of faith. But since the Church, from the time of Christ, has kept revelation and the means of grace free from error, it calls itself the One True Church. This means that without Christ no one can come to God, no more and no less. After the death of Christ the Church became the authentic protector that has kept the truth in an unbroken chain.

We are ashamed to have to emphasize that in no way is this a condemnatory judgment against an inquiring pagan or an erring evangelical brother. We agree with our evangelical brethren that the division of the Church can never be willed by Christ. He spoke of one shepherd and one flock, and His high-priestly prayer resounded with the repeated wish "that all may be one."

This knowledge obliges us to pray for unity. But it is not meet for our Catholic brethren to look down with pride and scorn on those in error, for "we wish to hate error but to love the erring."

When Frederick Wilhelm III mentioned to Count Leopold of Stolberg that he did not wish the people to be untrue to the faith of their fathers, the count replied: "I also, your Majesty; for that reason I have returned to the faith of our fathers."

Dear Lord, I have never yet thanked you for the gift of belonging to the true Church. I have often felt that being bound to it is a burden. I was too lazy to profess my faith, and I have sometimes smiled sympathetically at the zeal of the preachers of the sects. But in my Catholic self-assurance I have never realized that I ought to be, through my life and my words, the bridge to truth for my erring brethren. Forgive me this culpable negligence and let me announce your truth from henceforth.

CHRIST
and the Priest-workers

IN a north-German port I met a priest-worker for the first time. We were sitting at breakfast in the parish house when a French longshoreman, a giant in stature, knocked at the door. His ship had come in during the night, and he had just been shoveling coal. He looked haggard. With his big hands he searched his work trousers for his papers. He was a priest and he wanted to celebrate Mass. He had brought a sailor along as a server. In our comfortable house I felt very bourgeois and embarrassed.

This experience made me restless, so I followed the priest. I went to the place where the priest-workers were at home, to France. In the poor district of Paris I sought them out and spoke to them for a long time. I also found them in Bordeaux and talked with them through half the night to learn the secret and the meaning of their work. In Marseilles I lodged in the harbor district near them so that I could study their way of working. Soon I saw myself as a useless outsider and an importunate journalist, who wanted only an interview. Then I no longer made myself known to them, but in civilian clothes I followed them into the miserable barracks where they lived together with other workers. I have seen how, after a hard day's work, they celebrated the Holy Sacrifice in the evening—on a simple table in some back room near the communists.

At that time criticism against these men had long been in the air. Already in 1953 the sensational book of Abbe Gaudin had shocked conservative Catholic circles. People demanded the suppression of those agents of unrest.

But Abbe Gaudin was right. France had become a mission country. This statement was repeated by hundreds. The mission of Paris and the mission of France were soon started. These were two distinct movements. They were officially approved at Rome.

How did these priest-workers operate? It was not a question of building bridges from a bourgeois world into this French underproletariat of workers. They did not wish to be mere observers who would survey the lost position of the Church in the worker's world. They by no means wished to inject bourgeois politics into the heart of the working class. They soon saw that, sociologically, the world of the workers was entirely different. They wanted to place themselves in the midst of the workers and to become like them through a sort of "naturalization" in order to become all to all. That was a tremendous step. We are reminded of the holy experiment of the Jesuit, Ricci, who, centuries ago, wanted to become a Chinese to the Chinese. What would we have accomplished for the Universal Church if that effort, hindered at the time, had succeeded!

These priest-workers in France did not wish to stir up any excitement. But the press pounced on these "sensations" like a vulture, and undermined this pioneer work by false accounts.

To put it clearly: The holy experiment failed. It was stopped. It is understandable that these revolutionaries in priestly clothes were looked upon with mistrust. Not that they were suppressed because they were judged to be heretical. But the priest-workers in the midst of this underproletariat of workers, foreigners, North Africans, and Berbers, learned to make use of a terminology that sounded too much like Marxism. For in all kindness let it be said that they were too little prepared. They had learned to think only in the categories of their seminary days; they had been too much protected. Moreover, they were not physically strong enough to bear the hardships of a double vocation. One who works hard eight hours and lives in a shack, cannot during the night hours fulfill the tasks of a priest. This tragedy may have opened the way for many a priest safe in his office, and many a layman comfortable in his smug self-satisfaction, to say: "We knew that it would not succeed. We always warned against it."

To put it directly: No one of us has the right to criticize uncharitably this holy experiment. If the Holy Ghost worked anywhere, it was here with these men, who perhaps began thirty years too soon (or thirty years too late—if we no longer succeed in winning back the masses of working men).

Newer and better ways are being sought. We must give time to the men of intellectual and spiritual initiative to think these matters through and to prepare for them. May the right atmosphere be given to our young theological students to prepare for this mission!

But in spite of all well-founded and justifiable criticism, we shall be thankful to the French Catholics, who —as so often before—had the courage and immense boldness to dare an experiment that perhaps only later will see success.

Let it be said again to all pessimists in Catholic and communist camps: The work in this field is again in full swing. Men work day and night at a general plan that is being elaborated. Knowledge has been gained for this purpose and new attempts will be made to enable priests to become "all to all."

And there is great need for this. We have academic chaplains, student helpers, chaplains for soldiers and prisoners; yes, we have had priests as teachers and educators for one prince. Why then should not the widest sociological sector of a people, which through the influence of Marxism stands in the greatest danger of losing its faith, have its own priests? No one can deny them this right. Our prayer and our holy unrest must accompany these men, who in all quiet, according to the instructions from Rome, think and pray over this problem. The hearts of many zealous bishops will warmly support this work.

Will it not always be a bold venture?

Why have not the priests in Germany undertaken this pioneer work?

Did we not need it?

Let us not say in a spirit of vanity that we had no need. But the pastors of the Ruhr district had, thank God, other means of reaching the workers.

Nor did the workers of Germany desire priest-workers.

The social revolution in Germany did not effect an alienation of the workers from the Church as was the case with the French masses. Moreover, fifty percent of the theological students of Germany work in the factories during their vacations. For a long time societies of workers and Kolping families have been taking care of the German workers. During the last decades, worker-chaplains were made available to them.

And today, I am ashamed of the idle question that I, like many others, asked at that time: "What have you accomplished?"

You will understand this better from the following incident. It took place in a small French port. A young priest-worker, tired and haggard, came back from work. I was permitted to celebrate Holy Mass with him. He did this on a small garden table in his barrack house. After he had blessed the small circle of his fellow-workers and me, I asked him: "What have you accomplished by your work during the last three years?"

This was the wrong question. But it was typically German. It smelled of rationalism and Gallup polls. To become "all to all" does not call for speculating. It means to be able to wait, for here it is not a question of just making a few converts.

The priest-worker looked at me quietly and understandingly and said: "When I as a child of God go from the altar to the factory which is entirely communistic, when I stand there and work in God's name, then I have, through my presence as Christbearer, consecrated the red activity."

CHRIST
and the Clergy

FABLES about the clergy are far from dead, even though the heroic initiative of the French priest-workers and the chaplains in the concentration camps have made many people think.

Opinions about priests will always be divided. Nietzche wrote in "Zarathustra": "These priests irritate me and go against my taste!" But he wrote in another place: "Here are priests, and though they are my enemies, I pass over them quietly and with a sleeping sword. Among them also are heroes."

And so it will always be. The one spits on us, the other asks our blessing. German teen-agers tolerate me in my cassock as a relic of the Middle Ages—in London a girl greets me with reverence. One throws stones at us, another kisses our hands.

What is the reason for this? Do you think that priests are guilty? We do not deny it; there are blameworthy priests. The priest exists for a two-fold task. There are priests who, with the assurance of officials, merely fulfill their obligations and leave the Blessed Sacrament deserted. They have betrayed their royal priestly office for a kind of clerical fascism. We do not deny that there are priests who seek to equate their forgotten mission with an intolerance, even to private hobbies, whose prophetic task has died, and who announce an unpalatable threatening message, or who drip with salve and unction.

And there is the other type of priest, who indeed lives righteously, but who has become a spiritual automaton and soul-engineer, who without a soul cares for souls. Hebel was right when he said "that every crown will sometimes become a hat." So the holy vestment, the chasuble, has become a mere work uniform for such priests.

Do the majority of priests deserve the accusations that are made against the priesthood? By no means. For lax priests are, thank God, exceptions. At least I have known many more idealistic and holy priests than the other type.

Is it not interesting that the hatred of the Church's enemies is always directed first against *holy* priests? The fanatic brown-shirts did not first of all condemn those of the clergy who were mediocre, but they had a diabolical instinct for tracking down the fervent, genuine priests. These they killed.

How is this hatred to be explained?

Our Lord Himself foretold it. "The world will hate you as it has hated me." (John, 15:18) Christ Himself, the Most Holy One, on whom no shadow of Pharisaism fell, was persecuted even to the shedding of His Blood, and was finally nailed to the cross.

To the liberals of our day, Christ would be the prototype of a fanatic. Since they can no longer nail Christ to the Cross, they exercise their anticlerical hatred against His disciples, Catholic priests. And the more fervent priests are, the more vigorous are the persecutors.

It is a question primarily of these Catholic priests. All the other ministers of the two hundred and ninety-three sects, founded since the fifteenth century, may indeed be blameless men and have positions in society. But in this decisive religious controversy the Catholic priests stand alone. As witness to this we have the spate of novels and movies about priests, some good, others very poor.

There is an explicitly diabolic instinct that senses this mystery about Catholic priests. Perhaps Satan knows it better than the indifferent Catholic.

The Catholic priest, and he is alone, is "priest according to the order of Melchisedech"; one who, in place of Christ, exercises His power. (II Cor., 5:26)

With the first apostles at the time of Christ, with whom He is directly connected through the unbroken chain of ordinations, the youngest priest can say: "Let a man so account us, as servants of Christ and stewards of the mysteries of God." (I Cor., 4:1)

There is something wonderful and mysterious about these Catholic priests. God has, in a most literal sense, given Himself to these men. At every consecration the Lord of heaven and earth obeys the call of the priest.

God "needs" these men to distribute the graces of the sacraments.

In baptism this priest makes us children of God. He has the amazing power, with his "Ego te absolvo," of opening heaven anew to murderers. He speaks a blessing over the indissoluble bond of matrimony; he strengthens the dying with holy oil in their most difficult hour.

St. Teresa may have experienced this when she said: "If I should meet a priest and an angel, I should first salute the priest."

The ideal priest seeks no career; after long study he becomes a mere assistant, poorly rewarded. He knows no forty-hour week. He is a man of flesh and blood, feels like any other man, gives up marriage and family in order to live in the service of immortal souls, and to be a support to all the oppressed.

So the unceasing war of the atheists and half-atheists precisely against good priests is understandable: A priest is a prophet out of another world and for another world.

Therefore modern man in his metaphysical nonchalance must reject this "stronger one," who remains an outsider even when he is recognized socially as a "good fellow." He remains a "troublemaker" who, with his teaching about the other life, destroys the socialistic workers' paradise for the citizen of this world and causes it to collapse like a paper house—or at least he questions its value.

That is not all. In his black cassock he walks around like a living Ten Commandments, and he works in this pleasure-seeking world like a huge bird of death that presumably takes all joy away from men. With his Sunday Mass the pastor spoils the hard-earned Sunday outing, and with his gloomy insistence on the marriage laws upsets the "beautiful" concept of civil marriage. He disturbs the rest of those who are surfeited; he disturbs the activists by his teaching of eternal retribution.

Hence it is not the so-called bad priest who is the reason why the priesthood is so hated, nor is it the scandals that sometimes happen among priests. No one failed as sadly as Peter, the first pope, when he denied his Lord. But he wept bitterly, and Christ forgave him. Shall we not then forgive the sins and faults of those erring priests and bishops, who, in spite of their weak morals, at least did not betray the faith?

Of course we see the weaknesses of priests. But while the liberal enemies and the separated Christians point a finger at them or find in their weakness an excuse for their own soft and mediocre Christian lives, a faithful Catholic will listen and pray. Of course one notices a spot on a black cassock more easily than on a gray flannel suit. It is interesting that precisely this bad priest will be sought as a partner when it is a question of the affairs of God. And it is significant that Satan and his liberal party members make friends with this priest, and later seek to expose him. Indeed, this priest who has been made use of as spy will afterwards be dismissed with a kick.

The object of hate is the remains of the genuine Catholic priest, the one who is like Christ.

Voltaire cursed him.

But the world needs priests who, like the prophet Moses on the holy mountain, are mediators between God and the people—priests who give to the people not stones but bread; priests who, with consecrated hands, give blessings where the priests of Satan curse.

But all these considerations must not remain theoretical. Here a genuine examination of conscience and a concrete act must enter in.

Have you ever realized:

1. that through prayer, penance, and sacrifice you can help a disloyal priest?
2. that thousands of faithful Catholics observe Priests' Saturday with prayer and attendance at Holy Mass?
3. that in the solitude of the pagan big cities it does us good to be greeted, even as unknown priests, with a *Gruess Gott,* not with a cold *Guten Tag?*
4. that you could thank a priest orally or in writing for a good sermon, and thus recognize his efforts?
5. that one should never irreverently criticize the sermon, which is the word of God?
6. that one should pray for a priestly vocation among one's relatives?

And think of this: If a time should come when priests would be persecuted among us, would you be ready to receive such an "outlaw" secretly into your house and allow him to celebrate Mass in your living room?

Let us pray that that does not happen! It will depend, not least of all, on how earnestly you have taken these matters.

CHRIST
and the Yellow Peril

IN a German university city, I made myself available to the students for discussions. Good use was made of these opportunities.

What came out of it?

It was as it always is with the Germans. They were bursting with problems. But they did not approach them with the necessary seriousness. The religious theme was treated like a talk over tea and was little more than a flirtation with religion.

Inwardly I had to yawn—though I had to be tactful enough not to do so outwardly.

In the end I met a student whom I shall never forget—a colored Brahman of a noble caste of India, who was studying in Germany. Shy, almost embarrassed, he came in. "Father," he said to me in his broken German, "do you still believe in Europe?" I was taken unawares by this question and I gave no answer. He answered my silence: "I no longer believe; I have seen Europe and Germany."

Then he went out, but as he left he said: "Father,

pray for my sinful soul." (No young Christian student had ever asked for this.)

This episode should not be related as a sort of shock therapy. But one must be able to read the signs of the times. The facts must be taken seriously.

India and China, two giant peoples, are so densely populated that there is an earthquake in Europe when they shake hands.

India with its four hundred and fifty million people is taking an active part in the development of world history. Ghandi's idea of the non-violent revolution has not yet been extinguished. This country is in advent. Since the end of English domination in 1947, India has been seeking a new type of government.

A great vacuum has arisen for the Eastern peoples. The question now is whether communism or Catholicism will shape the destiny of these Asiatic nations.

That holds also for the Chinese.

The poorest illiterate in China is conscious of belonging to a people whose culture goes back many thousands of years. China has been much sinned against since its "discovery" by the Europeans. A Chinese coolie who works for an hour with his ricksha receives payment of a few pennies. We have no real conception of the plight of these men who live on a handful of rice a day —and hunger. The dictator, *hunger,* is worse than the present communistic dictator. He strangles millions of men with his bony fingers. And until now no power in the world has helped or wanted to help these people. Do we wonder that they now try it alone? The Our

Father petition, "give us this day our daily bread," is the same for them. Is it an injustice for them to pray thus?

A well-known man has said: "We must bombard China with wheat sacks." Yes, that would help. The whole world must join in helping, for China, by herself, cannot satisfy her needs. This action is not necessarily lucrative and will not bring much in return. In addition, the assistance must last for decades. But only in this way can the world crisis be dissolved. Communism has always had the knack of touching the sore spot and of offering itself as a liberator of the hungry and of the burdened. Do we wonder that now the Chinese accept this help and are tired of the empty promises of the "imperial nations?"

Besides, Europe has a debt to pay to Asia. Is it not a crime that England and America have kept open the channels for smuggling of opium? It is indeed not true that we have used germ warfare over China. But a much greater crime was done by the Europeans in infecting the Chinese with the opium vice. Moreover, the Chinese will not forget that during the English period signs were posted: "For Chinese and dogs this park is forbidden."

Injection of European poison has after effects. What have we brought to them? The methods for killing the unborn. We should rather have given them something to eat so that they could feed their children. In spite of that, they have far more births, which threaten the population of Europe politically.

The Yellow Peril! It is not here a question of Europe's annihilation hysteria. It would also be false to think that only Europe will be the victim. But it now depends on us to give an answer—otherwise communism will offer it.

With our electronics and our precision machines we will not impose ourselves permanently on the Asiatic peoples. They will soon make the same things, if they have not already caught up with us. A many-thousand-year culture will soon discover that behind the sky-scrapers of the West there lies a vacuum of the soul.

Neither will the hundred cathedrals of old Europe help. Do we really hope to accomplish anything in the Asiatic world, when a dozen or more sects are trying to sell their brand of faith? The rector of the University of Peking, who was educated in France, wrote in a student paper: "When a person goes to France without deeper knowledge, he may wonder at the many churches. But they are only the remains of a bygone and defeated epoch, which have been spared from the wrecking ax only for artistic reasons. In the same way we preserve in China artistic pieces of vestments of the Mandarin times, but nobody thinks of putting them on today."

This makes one think.

And yet, the greatest spiritual illiterates will no longer deny that the roots of all of today's problems are religious. It is so in North Africa, and it will be found true also in the East.

Because Bolshevism is at root a religious problem,

it will know how to speak to the Asiatic peoples in the right way. Shall we Christians bear the consequences of this?

A large number of the two thousand priests in China are in prison. Ninety percent of the churches are closed. The Christian missionaries have been driven out of China, and were lucky if they did not have to go through the terrible quarantine of many prisons beforehand. We will not help the tortured Chinese there with the imposing fleet maneuvers of the ships belonging to the "powers." Only the power of prayer and a fervent Christendom in Europe will be able to bring help.

What can we still do?

We cannot excuse ourselves by saying that China, for the present, is closed to us. (In spite of this, resourceful missionaries are able to get in.) There remains our task towards the Chinese outside. There are from eleven to twelve million in Europe who will be disillusioned by us. The urge for a Western education and a higher standard of living drives them to us.

They sit as students beside their white companions in our classrooms, while their homeland becomes politically vocal and takes its place in world economics.

The number of students from overseas is estimated at fifty thousand. In Germany there are three thousand, in France twenty thousand. These are the elite of Asia and Africa. The influence to which they are exposed is not a matter of indifference. The mission is made easy for us; we need not go to China.

But in reality how does it look?

The great expectations that these students have placed in Europe are not realized. If we do not take pains to avoid them, at least we are cool to them and uninterested. At best they are received at the port and helped materially, but then daily life begins for them. They receive no hospitality, and later on they are devoured by loneliness. So they become embittered and absorb the poison that they will some day pour out against us whites.

Even the Catholic students among them must feel that the cold shoulder is given them in our churches, that they are shut out; whereas at home they were accustomed to a warm family atmosphere. So these young men, hungry for kindness, must, in our Christian countries, experience a great feeling of abandonment. From one European country in recent years forty-four Catholics have returned to their Asian and African homes as apostates. Each one that we have lost is a lost battle for Christendom.

It seems that the communists are the only ones who have recognized their opportunities. With great zeal they receive the foreign students at the port of landing. They provide vacation camps and get-togethers. And it is only too understandable that these young men who cannot return home during vacation, and are often in financial need, cannot resist the invitation.

It is idle to ask what would have become of China if Tschu-En-Lai and Mao-Tse-Tung had taken different paths.

The fact is that both these great men studied in

Europe—Tschu-En-Lai in Gottingen, Mao-Tse-Tung in Paris. World history could have taken another path if they, for example, had had the experience that the Chinese priest, Father Huang, narrates to us: "I became a Catholic because in Europe I found a mother." And he tells the moving story of a fine peasant woman who received him as a refugee and took the last food out of her cupboard for him. Through her love he found his way to the Church and to the priesthood. Of Tschu-En-Lai, however, Father Huang had to say that he found no love. In Paris he was hired out as cheap labor. He was pushed aside as a social outcast of a less-worthy race. No one troubled about him. Tschu-En-Lai found no mother among us in Europe.

Hence, the Yellow Peril!

The following example may throw light on the situation. At a great institution I discovered in the audience a small Chinese priest. It may have been unwelcome, or at least surprising to him, when at the close, I asked him to bless us. I had just finished saying: "The Yellow Peril threatens us. Either Asiatic hordes will overrun us, or Chinese will come to us who are zealous for Christ!" It was then that this small Chinese came on the stage. He may have been frightened by the twenty thousand persons who stared at him. With his singing voice, that hung in the air like silk, he said: "Pray for my dear Chinese home." Then, with his thin voice, he prayed the Our Father in Chinese. He said the prayer for his Asiatic brothers. We all understood this warning.

CHRIST
and the Negroes

I should like to begin with the biography of a hero. Perhaps you have never heard of him, because he did not wage any war, nor did he receive any gold medals. He has become known to us as the "Apostle of the Negroes."

In 1610, a young student left his home in Spain and landed in Carthagena, the notorious and disease-ridden headquarters of the slave trade, where Negroes were sold like black ivory.

But this young Jesuit sought to atone for the sins of the Western world against these most unfortunate ones. He called himself Peter Claver, slave of the Negroes. This language was understood by the colored, who had known the whites, up till then, only as their merciless lords and persecutors.

The bed of Peter Claver was an ox hide; his pillow, a wooden board. Although his health was poor, he withstood the exceedingly hot sun and the stench and misery behind the ship's hatch. He was always there when smallpox, virus, diarrhea, and leprosy tortured these poor slaves. And when a runaway Negro was whipped to death by his lord, Peter stood like an angel beside him.

With these works of mercy, he plowed the ground for the seed of the gospel. To these despairing men, who were treated worse than animals, he preached a joyful message. And they heard and understood. If ten thousand colored slaves died without a curse for the whites on their lips, this man is to be thanked, who, as a hero and a saint, quietly and undramatically made the first breach in colonial narrow-mindedness and western arrogance.

You may think that this is a beautiful story, but that the Negro problem belongs to the past.

You are deceived. Have you not seen the newspaper accounts of what is happening in America, where segregation is a very serious problem?

There, three ladies beat a Catholic teacher because she was bold enough to instruct white and colored children together. The three were excommunicated. In another part of the country, a whole community was excommunicated because the people had refused to attend Mass on Sunday with the colored. That is how the Church reacts to such behavior.

If America is too far away from you, listen to what happened recently in an express train. A young father and his small son traveled with me. At a station a Negro opened the compartment door, looking for an unoccupied place.

"Oh, but he is black," said the little one. "Yes, close the door," said the father, "he bites." The child stared, disbelieving, and the grown-up smiled broadly.

What did this father think, and what do the many think who degrade the Negroes to bogey-men?

This Negro and thousands of others walk through our streets; they study among us, gather experience about the West, and understand enough German to grasp what one says behind their backs. We would be very glad to relegate the Negro problem—the colored problem in general—to the colonial and financial sphere. There, of course, it belongs in the first place.

The plight of the Negro draws a circle around the earth, through Africa, through America, but also through all the big cities of Europe.

The colored go into the gold mines of Johannesburg by tens of thousands. The large amount of money that they earn is soon taken from them by the whites. They are despised and herded together in Negro quarters. From the whites they learn only to drink and to make use of narcotics. We have not made them happier by giving them fat pay-checks, but we have lowered them to the level of work animals.

It is not to be denied that those responsible for the countries that have to solve the colonial question are faced with very difficult problems. There would be a social earthquake and a revolution as violent as anyone could imagine if Africa were to be emancipated overnight. It must be a gradual process. But "gradual" does not mean endless delay.

As serious as these financial-social problems are, the human problem is still more important. Or do we still have the small child conception of the "black man," as someone whom we must not come near? How then will we find a way to meet the thousands of mixed children in Germany if we accustom our children to point their fingers at their colored playmates and to consider them as animals from the jungle?

Our pure humanistic attitude will be scoffed at by many nations and races if we have not first solved the question according to religious principles.

It is very touching and beautiful when our children put their spare pennies into the box with the colored boy on it. It is good to "buy" a pagan child with five dollars; the child's instruction and baptism are made possible with this money. But it remains an empty action and a fanciful consolation to the good conscience of pious souls if we do not see in the Negro our brother in Christ, even though we never meet a colored person.

Christ passes through Africa. With His scourge He will strike not only this country where the most scandalous colonial and social sins are committed, but He will strike us also if we do not wish to be the protectors of our colored brethren. Indeed, the gospel alone will not convince the colored man. He has become distrustful —when one speaks of missions and in reality wishes to grasp political power. Our missionaries in Africa—those who, like Peter Claver, four hundred years ago, work untiringly to prove how Christ meant His joyful message—meet this distrust daily.

The warning complaint of a Negro poet should always sound in our ears: "When we return to God we shall tell Him how you have behaved toward us."

CHRIST
and the Military Camp

WE hate and curse war. One should not think it sinful of us when, after our experience, the military camp is an abomination to us.

We reject every type of military Catholicism which would like to help the Holy Ghost by using the sword. We wish no military fanfare in our divine service. We also do not believe in a military crusade against Bolshevism. One cannot place the kingdom of God and the kingdom of Satan geographically east and west.

No pope can sanction a war in which whole populations annihilate one another, but neither can any pope deny to anyone that self-defense which the natural law allows. No bishop may excommunicate a worthy policeman because he performs his duty with a revolver and protects someone from criminals. A soldier is a policeman against criminals from outside, when they attack a people.

And what does Holy Scripture say about soldiers?

There are no texts in Holy Scripture that condemn the vocation of a soldier. The Old Testament always recognized the duty of bearing arms. When Christ met the pagan centurion, He did not demand that he remove his uniform.

St. Paul carried on a religious discussion with the Roman legionary, and he did not condemn him because of his soldier's uniform. He saw in it no hindrance on the way to Christ. Even Luther answered affirmatively the question as to whether a soldier could be in a "blessed state."

And in the martyrology we find not a few soldiers and officers who have been raised to the honors of the altar.

All that has nothing to do with a naive flag-waving optimism, nor is it a question of military fanaticism. But it should be clear that a nation has the natural right and duty to protect women and children, home and culture.

The fifth commandment is: "Thou shalt not kill." That is, unjustly. Necessary armament and self-defense are not forbidden.

With soldiers and uniforms there is danger of war, yes; that they can bring it on is a tragedy about which we worry and tremble.

Even Christians are not free from this temptation. Who is to assure us that war-minded generals and business tycoons will not incite a war so that the old weapons may not become obsolete, or so that a new series of armaments may be manufactured with great profit, and that the tycoons may obtain for themselves new honors with the blood of our young men?

Proportionately, the Swiss have almost the largest army in Europe. And yet their last generations have not known what a war is, although the young men have their rifles in their cases.

"Never again a war!" This pathetic cry, among men affected by original sin and among Godless peoples, is just as naive as "Never again an earthquake."

But why should it not be possible that our nations, at least for one or two generations, should have peace and avoid war? Why should there not be in the nation officers who have no blood on their hands, and, recognizing the Ten Commandments, never make themselves guilty of war? Are we such pessimists that we no longer believe in the goodness of the soul of an officer and an armed people?

Indeed, the words "God with us" should not be borne theatrically on the military headquarters when religion is banned from the military camp. When the "instruction officers" teach a practical atheism and, instead of religion, offer a world-view watered-down substitute, then the war is already in the general-staff plan of the devil.

We shall not drive the recruits into divine service, although it would not be so terrible if a young ruffian in military service were led before his God.

Woe to our nations if officers rise up who cover a moral bankruptcy with dashing behavior. Woe if God does not form their conscience according to the Ten Commandments, even in the military camp!

We shall have to pray for officers who are ready to stand up in the spirit of the twentieth of July and protest when the inferno demands from them crimes of a despotic system and gives bloody commands which cannot be reconciled with conscience—and this, even if there is danger that such revolutionaries against a satanic order become martyrs. If we had had more of these generals who live the teachings of Jesus Christ, we could, after their execution, have honored their graves as the graves of martyrs.

"Lord Jesus Christ, our German people so easily tend to extremes. At one time it is a soldier nation to the last schoolboy; then again it is pacifist to culpable unpreparedness and rejects the arms that are necessary and permitted by God. Let us find the good middle way. You Yourself met the two officers who, as genuine soldiers, also embraced the faith. Give us officers who direct their conscience, not according to the war ministry, but according to You, the Lord, who brought peace to the earth."

CHRIST
and the Rosary Devotees

IT was not in Europe but in Mohammedan Africa that I had this experience: Men there said their prayers with such fervor that I cannot forget those praying Moslems in the streets of the Moroccan capital.

But you need not follow me to Africa. It was in Munich that, in the midst of traffic, a Moslem rolled out his prayer carpet on a public street, and with his face turned towards Mecca said his prayers with outstretched arms.

Your amused smile would probably have disappeared in the presence of his deep devotion. Similarly, you should never smile nor mock those who carry their rosary with them and are not ashamed to pray it publicly. Whoever makes fun of a praying man is not a gentleman; such a one lacks a most natural quality —reverence.

Perhaps I shall not convince you, but I should like to make you think by relating an experience that will always remain in my memory.

Of course there are numerous lukewarm Catholics who have their rosaries in their pockets like good-luck pieces, and are ashamed of them when some spiritual clod makes fun of them. But there are others, too.

We stood at attention in our battalion. The field sergeant was known for his party line and his senseless ridicule of all religions. Today he had a special trump. He dangled a rosary between his fingers and asked, grinning: "Who has lost this thing?" The predominantly Catholic battalion was suddenly a cowardly group. Even the men who had received rosaries from their mothers were silent. Only the color-bearer in the first row near me gritted his teeth and said: "If the fool does not stop his mockery, I'll punch him in the nose." I feared the worst.

The sergeant continued to mock, convinced that no one would call for the rosary. But my neighbor, the color-bearer, stepped forward, clicked his heels, and said: "This rosary belongs to me."

The battalion did not smile any more, and the sergeant could think of no fitting remark for the occasion.

I asked the young fellow afterwards: "Why did you not have the courage to ask for it at once?" "Because the rosary did not belong to me! But I wanted the fool to stop his mockery."

This fact later became known. The real owner of the rosary was discovered. From then on life in the battalion was made impossible for him. The color-bearer, on the other hand, was *the man*.

You see, it is not the most cowardly who pray the rosary. I could give you psychological arguments, although they would not explain the nature of the rosary. The fact that famous men, and field marshals like Tully, prayed their rosary, that the composer Haydn walked up and down and prayed a decade of the rosary while he created his greatest symphonies, that young men at the front held their mothers' rosaries in their hands and became heroes and saints while others broke down—all this does not explain the nature and value of the rosary. But it can make one think.

How can I convince you? Can I convince you of the love of a mother if you have never had a good mother?

Behold, Christ had a good mother. He gave her His devotion and He honored her.

An angel from heaven, announcing her mission, greeted her with: "Hail, full of grace." Until the end of time this greeting will be repeated in prayer. It is written in Holy Scripture, which our Protestant brethren also have.

Therefore the Church has always honored this mother. Not, of course, as a goddess. We do not give divine honor to Mary. That would be ridiculous. But we honor her as the greatest saint of all time. And that is why, throughout the centuries, there are Marian cities, and many thousands of Marian churches, into which people perpetually come to pray.

I do not forget the evangelical minister who said

in St. Paul's Church in Frankfort: "You should not smile at the honor given Mary by Catholics. If we had her, our churches would not be such cold ice-palaces."

Every mother celebrates her mother's day. Even the street woman, if she is a mother, is honored by her child. Should not we honor the mother of Christendom? The nations that no longer honor Mary are on the surest road that leads away from Christ. Even Luther, to his last days, preached about the mother of God on the Marian feast days.

Perhaps you could understand the praying of a single, slow Hail Mary, as a greeting, as the angel spoke it to her. But you ask how can one repeat the same thing fifty times, like a prayer mill?

You are right. Often it is a muttering without reverence. But do not be too quick to use that word "muttering." It is fifty times the greeting which the Son of God, through His angel, sent to His Mother. Can it be tedious for one to say a good, kind word to his mother fifty times? Just what is tedious? The mysteries of the rosary which accompany the Hail Mary are concerned with God. But God can never be tedious—only to the distracted person is the rosary tiresome.

Probably the unrhythmical but reverently-meant recital of the rosary by a village parish will open the gates of heaven wider than any theological discussions.

If our men prayed the rosary in the face of death, if our wives on the way to Russia held the rosary in their hands, if the dying can say it as their last prayer, then it must be more than sentimental babbling. Here there is nothing to smile at.

You wonder how a custom can have such value?

There are, in prayer-life, rare, moving hours, which break suddenly over a man like a local shower. But there is also something else: the steady rain that sinks in and is so much the more valuable. With this latter rain we should compare the rosary.

We know that with simple Catholics the rosary may have became a good-luck piece, like a teddy-bear charm or a silver amulet. But here, too, we must be careful with such a judgment.

We once experienced the mysterious power of the rosary when a beast of a Russian commander wanted to choose his victim from among a group of thirty girls. When nothing else helped, the desperate girls took out a rosary. Not that the commander would have prayed; he probably had no spark of faith any longer. But he looked at the rosary, started back aghast, and disappeared. With this great woman, Mary, he apparently did not wish to come into conflict. It was not only once, or in one place, that an episode like this happened.

You see, you should not smile at the rosary, but rather think reverently of it. The real believers, our mothers, have never given up saying the rosary. Even saints were formed through this prayer.

It will always be the custom to place a rosary in the hands of a dying Catholic. It is to be hoped that he has prayed it also during life, so that this final act may not be mere show. For dead, cold fingers the rosary comes too late.

Hence, try to understand those who pray the rosary. There are millions, and they are not the worst people.

The hand that holds a rosary will hardly throw a grenade at another. A man who truly prays to the Mother of God will never be able to trample on the soul of an innocent young girl. A woman who prays the rosary to the mother of all mothers will hardly murder her unborn child.

So at least we should have respect for those who obtain power and courage from the rosary.

Perhaps we can learn from two small boys who, for two years, had been the best friends, though they were not of the same faith. One day the Catholic boy lost his rosary at play. The other teased him and mocked him. The Catholic boy finally struck his companion in the face. Silence followed. It seemed that the friendship had come to an end. But the Catholic boy, ashamed, went to the other and said: "I must explain. My father had this rosary at the front when he fell. A fellow soldier sent it to my mother and me. And I pray with it and honor it as he did."

Try to honor your friend and neighbor who remains constant and full of courage in professing his faith, and who, with the rosary, sends the same greeting to the Mother of God that Jesus Christ sent to her.

The evangelical Goethe made Gretchen pray to the

Mother of God thus: "O thou who art rich in sorrow, bow down thy countenance graciously to my need! With a sword in your heart and a thousand sorrows you look down on the death of your Son. You look up to the Father, and you send up sighs for His and your need."

For us Catholics the Hail Mary is not a literary exercise, but a never-failing childlike prayer that our Russian brothers in Christ pray with us. "Hail Mary, full of grace, the Lord is with thee. Blessed art thou among women and blessed is the fruit of thy womb, Jesus."

CHRIST
and the Telphone Booth

ENTER a telephone booth. There you will find all kinds of numbers: the fire department, the doctor, the police, etc. That is as it should be.

But why is there no number there with which one might call a priest on behalf of an immortal soul, in case of a spiritual crisis? Everything is taken care of except the soul; it is forgotten.

It is sad that even I as a priest did not think of this idea. A young man, not even a Catholic suggested it to me. And the idea soon became a reality.

Among the twenty thousand listeners who came to a lecture in this big city, there were at least five thousand men who no longer knew the inside of a church. To them the priest smelled too much of incense for them to seek him. And yet, behind their smiling masks, there was so much confusion in their souls that they actually longed to meet a priest. That the idea was ripe was shown by the way it spread like fire.

On the very next day, in many telephone booths of

the city, there was to be found in large print the number: 22375. The priest-answering service was born.

For the metropolitan press this was an amusing idea which, unfortunately, they quickly reported. However, it helped us to publicize this number.

Every evening there is now a priest on duty under the number 22375. Anyone, without revealing his name, can call this priest and speak with him. The priest will consider the matter as in the confessional. Many have taken advantage of this opportunity.

True, the sensation-seeking reporters in England and America have tactlessly published that case in which a young man about to commit suicide received an answer that showed him the ultimate meaning of life.

That was the first call. Innumerable calls followed. They often came from despairing men who, in their need, sought a way out. They knew that on the other end of the line there was someone who had time and who understood them.

Only one person ridiculed me and insulted me through the mouthpiece. I answered him thus: "Friend, perhaps when you are dying you will call for a priest, and I do not know if one will be available."

The laughter at the other end stopped, and I hung up.

One may argue about this modern manner of caring for souls, but "It is better to light one candle than to curse the darkness." Isn't it foolish to condemn modern techniques and modern progress instead of trying to use all inventions for the honor of God? When the first cable was laid under the ocean to the U.S.A., the first message sent was: "Glory to God in the depths."

Perhaps Christians feel too much like owners. We feel too complacent in our niche and have no missionary spirit. We need a missionary blood transfusion from St. Paul to give us a modern, worldwide pioneer spirit. For that we need technical means.

As far as I know, no bishop still has an oil lamp in his house. The pope does not reject the telephone. No modern pastor could do so either.

Why should it be closed to the word of God? There are private lines for the diplomats, for the army, for committees—why not a line for heaven?

May the laity shame us if we priests are too tired or lack inventiveness!

For example, during a sermon, a postal official saw the overcrowded church and made a suggestion that a telephone line should be kept open and the sermon broadcast to other churches through a loud speaker. Thus it was possible for an additional four thousand to hear the sermon.

Perhaps it sounds improbable, but we should be glad that some time ago several girls at a post office asked their supervisor if they could listen to a sermon through the telephone. It was their only oportunity of hearing it.

"Young ladies, I do not see you; I only know that

you are sitting together and that you asked for a lecture." Thus I began a ten minute sermon over a telephone to a distant office.

It is true, as St. Paul says to the Romans, that faith comes through hearing. But how can men hear the good news if we do not bring it to them? And when they culpably remain away from church, we must not condemn them, but go after them.

Christ sought to meet men wherever He could. Today He would use the airplane and telephone to save a soul. He would presumably not live in a Syrian nomad tent, but in a modern house where He could use all the available means for saving souls.

Dear Lord, let me use all the things of this world in the right way. Engineers may not be priests of a modern world, but in the name of God they plan and construct and prepare inventions to develop what God has created.

The technique is not evil simply because murderers exchange views through the telephone, adulterers use it to make their rendezvous, and criminals discuss their evil deeds through it.

Let us without ceasing make known to men Your goodness and love, and to this end let us use the telephone and telegraph and put them at Your service.

CHRIST
and the Big-Business Men

DO you know the type? Faultlessly dressed; appropriate tie; well-pressed clothes; clean-shaven; aromatic cigars; best chocolate; brief case. Often on a journey in a Cadillac, in a Pullman or on a plane.

He appears at many conferences, at every trade fair.

So—or in similar circumstances—you have often seen him!

But do not think that only men with these outer marks are big-business men, that only the chiefs, the directors, and office managers are the executive type!

There are executive types in every calling. There are those who have studied and those who have not, among civil servants as well as among laborers. There are male and female executive types; secular and religious, those who are V.I.P.'s and those who are not; all nationalities. Most often, of course, one finds them in business circles.

The executive is a type. The spirit of big-business is a certain inner attitude. It is a single-minded devotion to business in every form!

Hence it stands alone and is not burdened with any antiquated religious tradition. In religious questions the executive type calls himself neutral. (In business, indeed, he is not neutral, but often radical and, when necessary, brutal.) He obtains his religious ideas from newspapers and tabloids infected with "intellectualism."

On his all-too-frequent business trips, he takes off his conscience as if it were a garment. He manages and deals with money. Money rules his world. Coolly he reckons profit. He is better acquainted with the stock market than with the Bible.

He uses his power in every walk of life—without consideration for others. He has no inhibitions. Anything goes in his so-called private realm. He seeks relaxation in any place, from the lowest dive to the most exclusive nightclub, and sometimes exchanges his wife for his secretary or his servant.

He needs these amusements as narcotics because he is afraid to rest. Always driven on and busy, he drives others. His eyes go automatically to the clock. He never has time for anything except business.

The tragedy is—he has no time even for God. But he is no atheist. (Satan himself is not that.) But for him, God is not substance, not reality. He is not even business for him. He overlooks God. But God does not overlook him.

God has made an important appointment for him. It is the meeting to which God calls him after death.

On the police news one hears the report. "On Stuttgart-Munich road last night the car of Mr. ---- crashed into a bridge pillar. It is thought that he was over-tired. He was killed outright."

Moreover, when the police arrived, the stock market news was still coming over the undamaged radio of the otherwise demolished car.

So the business man drives to death and judgment, at which his best lawyer can no longer help or defend him. At most, the prayer of someone, perhaps his own child, can help now. The prayer for which he never had time. A prayer at which he may have smiled, or even cynically mocked.

He had to retain much in his head, and he knew by heart many accounts, as well as the value of stocks. Did he think in time of his account in eternity? That alone is important now.

Business men of the twentieth century are the product of our technical age—but the problem two thousand years ago was the same. Even then they had a counterpart. He was overly busy with building-plans and fanciful affairs. And Christ said to him: "You fool, yet in this night they will demand your life from you!" This text is so important that you must read it for yourself.

Or are you one who finds no place in your daily schedule for the reading of Holy Scripture? You will find this important passage in the Gospel according to St. Luke. (12:16-23)

And recite the following prayer, now—otherwise, like

your counterpart, you may at some time be prevented from prayer by sudden death.

Dear Lord, in some way we are all in danger today of becoming big-business men—weary, driven by appointments, seeking after profit. But do not let me forget the one appointment and the one necessary thing. This appointment is not yet on my agenda, but You know it already. Let me think of it at all conferences, meetings, and business dealings, that I may be able to stand before You at the final judgment. Otherwise all the rush and work of my life are senseless and worthless in the light of eternity.

CHRIST
and Paragraph 218

THE complaint has been made that we consider the Bible only as a book of edification for pious souls. Dreaming humanitarians, at best, take out a few fitting ethical or literary crumbs. That Christ is the Son of God they deny because of the consequences to themselves. With tolerant, benevolent countenances they honor Him as one who makes the world better, if they do not, in a sentimental moment, degrade Him to the rank of a tolerant side-stepper. Unfortunately, there are enough lame Christians who, with piously elevated eyes, dish out the words of the Bible as if they were sugar-cookies.

But now a question for you. What are you going to do with the words of Holy Scripture? Please read a chapter of St. Mark. Do not let me cite it, but read it yourself. I refer to the passage in verses 42-49 of the ninth chapter.

The story there is frightening. It is the story of a man, around whose neck a millstone is to be hung if he scandalizes a child. Did you hear? Only a matter of scandal! What must the punishment be if he murders a child?

But for that there is a paragraph in the German criminal law. It is the notorious Number 218. We Christians need no such paragraphs which are, after all, well worn and full of holes. For us the fifth commandment is enough "Thou shalt not kill!" But where one no longer recognizes the Word of God and His commandments, and where one seeks to put in order a godless world by means of a penal code with ineffective laws, Number 218 is a nonsensical device with which the people bring ruin upon themselves.

In Germany and Austria we must shut one ear so as not to hear the death clock striking for our families. Soon we shall have more coffins than cradles. It is bad for a nation when garbage dumps become cemeteries for unborn children. True, it is not always so brutal. For "humane" doctors and quacks know how to perform the crime of abortion very nicely.

Since it is not a question of human laws, but of an important commandment of God, all violations of this paragraph are sins against the fifth commandment of God, crying to heaven for vengeance.

At first medical arguments are used. We laymen may be considered ignorant, but we know from very talented doctors that the "medical diagnosis" has become, with few exceptions, an alibi for irresponsible doctors with bloody fingers. They ooze humanitarianism when they "help" a woman.

We know that in Europe there are societies for helping mothers, organized by the state, that have become unofficial murder institutions.

Indeed, Russia did not halt its death caravan on ethical or religious grounds. It is now trying the bloody experiment again, temporarily, in spite of a former edict.

Austria has become the morgue of Europe. Its statistics must open the eyes of even a shallow-thinking layman. Even the uneducated can no longer be deceived by the medical mumbo-jumbo which denies that there is any danger in abortions. For the most skillfully performed medical abortion is, in any case, more harmful than a difficult birth. Such an attack affects the body like a pitcher of cold water thrown on a hot plate. Whoever places the terrible phantom of death before a mother about to give birth should be told: "If at birth one mother dies, there are two or three times as many mothers who die sooner or later because of abortions, not to mention the bodily injuries that are caused. We have no illusions about the meaning of those numerous vague announcements: 'She died in the flower of youth.' "

Death in the maternity ward is much spoken of, but in auto races, in circuses, in mines, and in every other walk of life, it is taken for granted. Our secular generation cannot understand that it can also be part of a mother's vocation to become a "martyr" for her child. A mother who dies for her child appears before God as a saint or a martyr, but those who die from abortions appear as murderers.

Where the medical diagnosis does not succeed, some like to bring in Paragraph 218 along with the economic argument. The phantom of overpopulation and world famine is scientifically too vague to be accepted. We cannot deny that the population of the world has climbed immensely. Two and a half billion men live on the earth. But this earth could nourish two to three times as many men if we did not spend huge sums for making weapons, if we built large research institutes to seek out the unimagined riches of the earth and of the sea in order to convert them into food, and if the stockbrokers and auctioneers would stop limiting world-wide charity to what looks good on a profit and loss statement. At any rate, one cannot solve the problem by murdering children under the slogan of "birth control." Did America not incur great guilt in this way among the Japanese?

False compassion would like to undermine Paragraph 218 through social diagnosis. Lack of housing, poverty, and all the many social ills should not be underestimated here. But they must never be made an excuse for child murder. A reasonable social program must give help in this matter.

Since 1933, the eugenic argument, the prevention of the increase of hereditary diseases, recalls too many bloody memories to need refuting again.

In the eternal struggle about Paragraph 218, medical, economic, or population considerations may be important. But they remain rooted in materialism. They do not consider the soul. But it is precisely the soul that ought to have first place in all these arguments. For the soul of a child is worth more than all the treasures of the earth. And the soul of a woman who has been trampled under foot is more tragic than a system of disturbed suns in the universe.

The whole tragedy of a crime against Paragraph 218 strikes at the region of the soul. One may deceive the law, but guilt before God remains. Anxiety and guilt are like phantoms, from which these women never free themselves.

But please do not say that the Church has caused this anxiety complex in our women. That is not true. In the northern countries, for example, where they are almost chemically free from all church influence, the state has "sanctioned" this crime. The state churches are also silent, and indirectly allow this sin. So the anxiety complex cannot come from the Church. Nevertheless, those who give psychotherapy, as well as nerve doctors, are over-worked. Why? Why is the suicide rate so high in these socially model countries?

Because, besides the state's rubber stamp decrees, there are also the unchangeable laws of God, which cannot be violated with impunity.

Do not believe that you can ignore these state, political, and theological considerations. For all of us, though we are not directly involved, have, in some way come into collision with Paragraph 218. We dare not complain against the guilty with the voice of a judge.

The woman and the girl who in their despair find no other way out are not alone in their guilt.

We are all murderers:

- the lawmakers, who wish to sanction abortion;
- the doctor, who gave the tablets in the fourth week;
- the druggist, who was ready to help;
- the landlord, who says that after the third child the family must move out;
- the friend, who knew the address of "a friend of a friend";
- the mother, who out of anxiety and because of shame urged her daughter to have an abortion;
- you and I, who have kept silent, or who, with a full cupboard, were unwilling to help outfit a new crib.

A MOTHER'S PRAYER:

Dear Lord, You know I will never commit the crime of abortion. But my health is poor, and our two rooms are so small. My husband earns little, and our three children have scarcely the bare necessities. Let me find a way so that I may not lose the love of my husband, but also that I may not injure Your love, O God, by a serious wrong in marriage.

CHRIST
on the Assembly Line

A GROUP of Spanish workers proclaimed that working on an assembly line is contrary to the dignity of man. This protest may make an impression. But it remains an anachronism and in our age sounds romantic and repetitious! Unfortunately—or shall we thank God?

We Christians always believe in progress in the best sense, and we wish to affirm all that is implicit in the Scripture text: "Make subject the earth."

How is it with the assembly line?

It is known that as early as 1910 the assembly line was used in the slaughter houses of Chicago, and that since then it has taken over all large industries. Can one consider it as merely monotonous, mechanized, soulless work? That would be showing too much resentment. One can hardly compare a modern assembly-line worker with a galley slave of antiquity.

Why should man's strength not be spared when it can be fully replaced by the machine and the assembly line? When in that way the too-long work period of harrassed man is shortened? One could, if he liked, add more to the praise of the assembly line.

And yet Christ would be shocked if He should see these modern workers in the factory. Not that a worker's soul can be caught in the wheels of the machines, but there are enough causes for alarm in this matter which even the greatest optimists can no longer ignore. What is to become of a spiritual man on the assembly line when, after two to three weeks of practice, he reaches the peak of competence, as, for example, in the great Ford works in Detroit? The most ignorant person can learn his task in a few days. But the man remains no thinking personality; he becomes merely a part of the machine. In the gigantic system of the factory, the workers are only cogwheels; there is no teamwork, no working together. Activity of the soul, like that which a craftsman or artist experiences, is lacking.

But when one asks the workers in these factories if they are satisfied, the answer is often in the affirmative. And they are even so content that they do not wish a change from this monotonous work. But precisely this satisfaction makes one perceive a sickness, namely, a dangerous spiritual anemia.

From this, one cannot explain the desire which, after the vacuum of the working hours, seeks satisfaction in games of chance, brutal sexuality, and uncontrolled pleasure-seeking.

It is not as though these things remain hidden from the big-business man; not as though leading men had not tried to help! But the therapy has not increased in proportion to the ailment. Humanizing the assembly-line work, lessening the strain, providing bodily comfort, and work hygiene, sports facilities and the like, may heal much of the sickness of the assembly-line workers. But these remedies do not touch the deep-seated infection.

One can help in many ways with such well-meant humanitarian reforms, but these things do not touch men's souls. Their souls must continue to rust and spoil. Yes, it almost appears that under the best working conditions and in the hygienically unobjectionable factories, a process takes place in which man is robbed of the last chromosome for God. In such rooms religious oxygen is lacking. The result is that the worker becomes a robot, though he may be a highly qualified robot, equipped with reverse action.

With all our testing methods and Gallup Polls, we shall not be able to lessen this sickness. If we do not confront our assembly-line man with Christ, he is lost. For only through Christ does the smallest pin in the over-sized workshop recognize his own personality—that which raises him out of the production line and puts him face to face with an all-powerful Creator-spirit.

Such a religiously-minded man will seek his strength and recreation not in merely superficial distractions and pleasures, but will create activities out of deeper sources. This alone will enable him to make himself a thinking and responsible master of the super-mechanized work process. And only such workers will have the courage at the given hour, in the name of their immortal soul, to become revolutionaries against a development through which man will be forced to give up his soul at the gate of the factory, along with his pass.

PRAYER AT THE ASSEMBLY LINE:

Dear Lord Jesus, You have taken on Yourself all the sufferings of Your time. But from one suffering you were spared. You have never experienced the soulless work of the assembly line in which I have been mercilessly placed. But in Your divine providence You have permitted my work. Give me the grace that I may not lose my soul at this spiritless activity. When the spirit lies broken, let me so much the more lift my soul to You and open it to my brother.

CHRIST
and the Golden Children's Village

WE are building a golden children's village! And we pray to You, O God, for Your blessing. The village consists of small houses, in which women with practical ideals take the place of mothers, one for each group of eight children.

But what is one village for so many homeless children? The earth has room for all, and people build extensively. But Your dear ones, Lord, are so often suffocated by the narrow, loveless self-interest around them.

We build skyscrapers with sunny suites of rooms—yet tens of thousands of refugee children vegetate in confining barracks. We build comfortable villas—but more dogs than children play in them. We build worldly casinos in which the dice roll—but many of our little ones have not even a ball for their innocent play. We build luxury hotels for men who do not know how they will spend their time or their money—but outside the windows plead the sad eyes of imprisoned children, children for whom the street becomes home because their parents, busy at work, have no time for them.

We build dog houses, and animal clinics; animals are loved—but thousands of youngsters should come before the dogs, because *they* have *no* home. We build sports stadiums; so friendly are we to men—but small houses, because they lack space, become coffins for unborn children. We build modern factories to worship the standard of living as a god—but in many young marriages the child must wait; and sometimes he is sacrificed to this god. We build movie palaces for the amusement of the masses—but thousands of children know no other playground than the alleys in the big cities. We build luxury express trains for extravagant vacations—but in our vacationers' kingdoms children are apt to be seen only in third class.

Yes, Lord, men build and build. But Your dear ones, the children, suffer and waste away. The world has no room for them. Reward all those who have given even one stone to build a home for these little ones in our golden children's village, and bless the courageous women who take the place of mothers for our orphaned children.

But let us not tire when the difficulties overwhelm us and we are threatened with suffocation by misunderstanding and red tape. And let us never forget that the children are Your loved ones. You have blessed them and said: "Whoever receives one of these little ones receives Me."

CHRIST
and the Feeble-minded

AN appendectomy today means nothing. But stomach cancer is frightening. Multiple sclerosis? Unthinkable! Please do not torture the healthy with the thought of it! Perhaps one does something for his sick neighbor, pays a short visit and brings a bouquet of flowers. But more than this cannot be borne by the highly-strung man of today.

Outside the city, in the midst of a great park, there stands a house, no—a little city; there one finds no knockers on the closed, padded doors. There dwell the feeble-minded, the insane. Their spirit is dark; it is as night, a mockery of the "crown of creation," an insult to the image of God. How does that little city look? Terrible!

One door after another opens and closes behind us. There they stand and sit around, looking at us out of empty or unfriendly eyes. They follow us, smiling like children or brutes, they run, cry, and then sink back into rigidity. They were once healthy like you and me. God knows more reasons than the psychiatrist why they ended here. A big young man strikes with his fist against the lattice; he strikes till his fist is bloody. He shouts, "Take me along!"

"He recognized you as a priest," says the caretaker. "That is a confrere of yours." In the war a wound in the head, a piece of shrapnel, a priest becomes an insane person!

Are you afraid of that last door? Inside you will find the idiots who learn nothing and can do nothing but eat and sleep; the deformed who are washed and fed like captive beasts. They never get out of their small beds; they are bound to them, because they are as dangerous as wild animals.

You are frightened. You cannot grasp that. So you were right with your annihilation theory which states that some creatures are unworthy of life. Would it not be merciful to destroy them? How can a man believe such an idea? It is true that pagans before the time of Christ could not do it, and the pagans after Christ are still less able. If after death there is nothing, it makes no matter whether one cuts off the life-thread of the insane sooner or later. Isn't that so? Why should a people, a state, burden itself with such expensive and unproductive citizens?

How does the Christian react? Christ came and He did not pass such creatures by. He even healed the man who was possessed by the devil. Once He destroyed two thousand swine for the sake of one soul. This one soul, even if it be that of a sinner, is worth more than the whole universe.

Indeed, even he who wishes to explain human existence in terms of animal life, saying that we are no more than intelligent animals, cannot explain away Christ's attitude in the matter. He should be careful that he does not lose his own understanding on account of the senselessness of his life!

One can deny the soul—although today it is more fashionable to analyze it—but one cannot kill it; it is immortal. God created it as He created the body. Woe to the murderers who propose to tear this life out of the hands of God!

Do you see where we end up with our false compassion? It is an easy route from there to the gas chambers and to the other mad annihilation practices of the godforsaking dictators.

There is no unworthy life. Before God every man is worth an eternity, even if he is a pitiful image of human beauty and of the human spirit. You cannot be a Christian and deny these facts.

God has unimaginable powers. He can give to an insane person, in the blink of an eye, a chance to make the decision that normally takes a whole lifetime—the decision to reject evil and love God, and thus know Him for eternity in His glorious and unimaginable beauty. What do we know of such matters?

But to us Christ will address that stern rebuke: "What you have not done for the least of my brethren, you have not done for me. Depart from me."

Thou, Creator of all life! Thou knowest what our feeble-minded are in this age of progress:

to the loveless an object of scorn;
to the aesthetes a discord in the harmony of creation;
to the intellectuals a waste product to be ignored;
to the philosophers a disgraceful stain on the picture of mankind;
to the philanthropists a temptation to murderous compassion—reason enough to kill them.

In our veins also runs the poison of contempt or of unregulated compassion.

Help us to think rightly, so that we may seek Your image in the most pitiful of your creatures, and recognize the fact that their life is sacred. You have given us a clear, healthy intelligence, for which we must thank You daily. Let us never misuse it against You.

CHRIST
at the Race Track

IT is in the air, this fever, this strain, this driving excitement. One affects the other. Reporters, who hang on the heels of sensation, police warnings, drink-hawkers, and I know not what.

Men press together on the curves in restless groups and strain their necks to see. Some have rented a bus; others got up early to catch the chartered train in order not to miss the event.

No prayer, no blessing! Why should there be?

Antiquity called on the gods.

Today destiny lies in the hands of the directors and technicians. The machines are carefully tested; the drivers are hardened like iron.

Foolish to think that God. . . .

The cars rush on. Hellish noise—the others follow in seconds; they come, approach one another—then, a crash! screeching of brakes, splinters, horror!

Then a crowd of people. Police, doctors, reporters, stretchers, microphones! At once everything is at the spot of the accident. Whoever is not disturbed enough to move away stands gawking; after all, they have paid; they wish to take in this sensation also.

No one thinks about a priest. Of course not! What would Christ be doing on the race track? For these worldly masses, God is an exiled God.

Soon the dead man is pushed aside. The pools of blood are strewn with wood shavings as in a slaughter-house. The wounded are taken away. The race goes on.

Who thinks of the immortal soul of the one who raced to death? The doctor understood his work; he verified the death—nothing more!

The crowd is pagan. The cigarette sellers now sell delicious extra articles, and a bottle of coke tastes good after the shock; but the "article," God, is not sought. No one here at the race track thought of Christ.

No one? O yes, a young boy scout, who enthusiastically followed the race and knew every driver and every make of car—he kneels and says an Our Father for the dead driver.

Christ at the race track? He was there in this youngster.

Dear Lord, death lurks not only at the race track. Hundreds die today on the streets.

There are thousands dying every year. We tremble before the beast of war, and yet daily more are sacrificed to the false god, the auto: fathers of families, who go cheerfully to work and do not return; playing children, whom the street gives back to their mothers, dead.

Lord, in traffic, let me have respect for the life of

my neighbor so that I may not some time, because of my lack of consideration, bear the brand of murder on my forehead.

And the dead on the street, Lord, let them rest in peace!

CHRIST
and the Sick

DO not say that the Bible is a collection of dusty papyrus rolls from the East. It is as warm as blood—and it is living. Read in the fifth chapter of the Gospel according to St. John, verses five to nine. There you will find the story of the man who was sick for thirty-eight years, who sat and waited at the pool of healing—until Christ came. To Christ the sick man said the well-known words, in which all the bitterness of thirty-eight years was pent up: "Lord, I have no one to put me in the pool when the water is moved."

And do you think that this story in the Bible is no longer pertinent? These words: "Lord, I have no one" —has no one spoken them since then?

Think then . . .

—of the man with multiple sclerosis, who can no longer move himself, whom his friends have avoided as a leper for four years;

—of the tubercular patients, who are moved from one sanatorium to another, and who never even receive mail;

—of the blind, whom no one leads across the street, and to whom no one reads a newspaper or a book;

—of the lame, whom no one takes in a wheel chair into the sunshine;

—of the thousands of sick, the despairing, who are in this condition because no one cares for them.

They all complain like their companion in suffering two thousand years ago: "Lord, I have no one."

But do we not have well-organized groups providing care for the sick?

Of course, very good indeed! All is organized. But the love is dead.

We have modern hospitals. All is sterile—but hearts are also sterile. Or do you think that, besides providing the money for the sick—the operation, the medicine—there is nothing left to do?

We pay taxes and are satisfied that we have developed our welfare state so far.

So far, that out of thousands of windows the same complaint is to be heard: "Lord, I have no one."

So the word from the Gospel according to St. John is still true and is even more sad today, for Christ no longer goes through the streets of our big cities to give to these sick the saving answer.

Truly no more?

Well yes, Christ *does* go through the streets when we, like Him, meet the sick. Not cold functionaries, but a handful of saints will change the world. And if we do not all help one another, an ice age of hearts will come over us in a society without love.

When our women cry out that terrible word of Lucifer: "I will not serve," then in our souls we shall all freeze together.

Lord and Master, You healed many sicknesses on earth. But You have not taken sickness away from us. With our sick brothers and sisters, You give us a task for all time. Give to us who are healthy a restless heart, so that we may not close our eyes to our sick, but may lighten their suffering and their bitter loneliness by our helpful deeds.

CHRIST
and the Horoscope

FROM a Frenchman comes this bold announcement: "I await the Cossacks and the Holy Ghost."

That is no lame resignation, but Christian realism and unconquerable optimism. We mean the same thing when we say: "Even if mountains crack, we Christians will laugh."

On the other hand, what is to be said of the modern horoscope hysteria? The popular saying is right: "When faith has gone out of the door, superstition comes in through the window." It happens to men and women, to rich and poor, to the educated and the uneducated. There are betting-windows and state lotteries. These are only some of the peripheral outgrowths. And even the little man on the street is ensnared. There are amulets and talismans to bring good luck—charms, mascots, horseshoes, gilded clover leaves, and other similar things. A wave of childish foolishness has spread over the land, drawing millions of men.

In a large city of the Christian West, every fourth person goes to a "missionary of superstition." Fortune-telling, horoscope-reading, astrology, and the like, are his "sermons." What difference does it make to ignorant men that in many newspapers the horoscopes contradict one another, and that the most stupid platitudes are served up as "scientific"? People, it is said, do not believe in them; but they are ensnared by them. A man studies his horoscope every day, every week, and directs his undertakings and his business according to it.

Advertisers even make use of astrological calendars and brochures to attract attention. There are even astrological marriage bureaus which do a thriving business.

It is still worse when this goes beyond a private hobby. When the deceptive but clever superstition of astrology and of charlatanry has taken hold of a statesman, who, guided by the constellations of stars, leads a nation to war (These are historical facts!), then appears the devilry which embraces mankind because it has fallen away from faith.

Is there no relation between the constellations and man's history?

There may be certain cosmic relations that have an influence on man. Of that, however, only exact science can tell us, not the horoscope in the popular almanac.

But whatever relations may be effective, we know that divine providence rules over all stars, and that God has given us a free will. The Christian does not believe in predestination in the Calvinistic sense, nor in "fate," nor in Kismet. We know that we are in God's hands.

We know One Who has His own "horoscope." As

Son of God, Christ has foretold things that have happened precisely on the hour and on the minute. His horoscope was indeed terrible according to man's opinion. Contrary to all the messianic hopes of the Jews, He took upon Himself suffering and death according to the will of His Father. And he did not hesitate to call the first pope, St. Peter, Satan, because, in his human ignorance, the apostle wanted to oppose God's plans.

Suffering and even death are, for us Christians, no catastrophe. The way of every Christian is pointed out by His Master on Good Friday and Easter. Suffering also belongs to this way.

What the world calls bad luck is for us divinely-sent suffering, and what the world calls "blind destiny" is for us the fatherly hand of God, which leads us kindly even in the darkest hours.

How tranquilly and nobly men go through life who trust in the words of Christ. "Are not five sparrows sold for two farthings? And yet not one of them is forgotten before God. Yes, the very hairs of your head are all numbered. Therefore do not be afraid, you are of more value than many sparrows." (Lk., 12:6-7)

Thus our kind Father has best prepared our calendar for the coming year.

It is now up to us to follow our horoscopes, and thereby suffer uncertainty and anxiety; or to entrust ourselves with a free YES to God's plans. Then we can say with reason in the apocalyptic days: "I await the Cossacks and the Holy Ghost."

CHRIST
and the Spinsters

PARIS. One of the numerous street cafes. A pretty Parisian orders coffee. A young man sits at her table with unconcealed interest in her. She is lovely and modest. He invites her to go for a walk. They start to go out together. Then he notices that she limps. He grabs his hat and runs after the next bus, saying, "Pardon me, I forgot an appointment."

Will she be numbered among those who never know the happiness of marriage? Perhaps. In that case she will be among those who are left waiting, and she will have the title of "Old Maid."

Our super-enlightened age is pleased to leave behind ancient prejudices, yet this psychological misjudgment of spinsters is apparently not to disappear, immature and deeply wounding though it is.

The unmarried are considered purely biologically, and are regarded as nonentities. We look at their destiny materially and see their existence as full of uncertainty. We look at them statistically and alarm them with the six-figured number by which women outnumber men.

We consider them psychologically and give them even deeper inhibitions.

The problem of the unmarried is not an unaccountable phenomenon; it was the result of the war that forced this fate on millions of women. But the statisticians prophesy good prospects again for our young ladies.

There will always be unmarried women (and not only because some men are woman-haters.).

You really do not believe that millions of women remain unmarried because they are not pretty, because they are not clever enough, or because they lack domestic capabilities? The contrary is the case. The "cute" girl with plenty of sex appeal, but with more ignorance, will often be married very early; whereas to plain girls with golden motherly hearts, the happiness of marriage may be denied.

The fact that these girls may be otherwise occupied is no compensation to them. Do you wish to console the girl by pointing to something which she has accomplished: that she cared for her aged father until his death, that she supported her brother and educated him, or that she waited and worked like a slave until her five younger brothers and sisters were taken care of?

Who speaks of this forced celibacy that millions of women must accept?

Woe to us priests if we have no answer for these worthy women, or if we consider them as a necessary evil!

If the pagans were able, because of their religious beliefs, to esteem virginity (the Romans punished the vestal virgins by death for losing their virginity), how much more should we Christians esteem the virtue!

But the pitiful Christian western world has betrayed virginity, and too often approves of, or even applauds, the promiscuous woman.

Our very air is infected by this reign of dirt, and thousands of unmarried women who wish to recognize a vocation in their state, would not recognize it if Christ had not spoken so clearly. Not just once, but ten times Holy Scripture refers to the value of virginity. The martyrology, the Church's book of heroes, places before our eyes every day the greatness of this state, which modern materialists and the spiritually blind no longer appreciate or understand.

Indeed, there is no obvious solution to this problem, even if an unfortunate woman allowed herself to be advised by ten holy priests, they could say little to help her. She can solve it only with God. This solution lies enclosed in the one big YES with which the Mother of God gave herself to the will of God. The answer sounds simple and may deceive some of us. But there is no other.

There is also no substitute in having sexual relations, as the mistress of a married man. That is a sort of prostitution that can end only in tragedy. That virginity injures the health is just as much a fable as the claim that the personality cannot fully develop without sexual life.

It is not true that we have too many women in the world—we have too many "dames," but unfortunately too few motherly women. If only our unmarried women would understand what power they could wield if they cultivated love and warmth for cold mankind.

But they need to fulfill themselves in a motherly way. There are in all ways of life unmarried women who are ten times mothers among the children and the sick of their relatives and neighbors—while some married women enjoy their marriages selfishly and avoid all the responsibilities of motherhood.

But there are too few of these motherly individuals. The ruins piled up by self-love and egoism blockade for many women the only way to freedom. Others, who without marriage are fulfilling their high vocation, should know that they are not just "surplus women" in the sight of God.

CHRIST
and His Best-seller

I NO longer remember in what big city it was. The vendor at a newspaperstand praised with a hoarse voice "the most widely-read book in the world." I was curious. One must read a best-seller. I bought one. What did he place in my hand? Holy Scripture!

At what are you astonished—the originality of the newspaper vendor or the fact that the Bible is the most widely read book in the world?

Perhaps you did not know it. The Bible is translated into more than one thousand languages, some of which are known only to experienced language specialists. Before there were printed Bibles—and the Bible was the first book printed—hundreds of monks during the Middle Ages spent their lives copying the Book of Books. Hermits spent decades with this book alone, and saints have read it on their knees.

Once, an oriental prince was on a journey. He loaded a dozen camels with the most important books from his great library. But the route through the desert was too difficult; so he had to have half of the books unloaded. When the remaining books were still too troublesome to transport, he again had the most important ones sorted out. Finally, there remained of his giant library one lone book. This book alone seemed worthwhile to him and satisfied him. It was the Bible.

What about this book?

The fact that in America an old Bible translation was insured for one and a half million dollars for a ninety-minute trip, and was obtained from the bank treasury under police guard—that is sensational and interesting.

To have the priceless original text kept in the museums of Rome and London—this could make the learned enthusiastic. Such honor concerns only the age of the books. But what must it mean when our men, on their way to Siberia, tore this book apart so that each one might have and read one page! When our priests in Russia wrote Holy Scripture from memory on tree bark because there was no paper. When our prisoners fastened it with a nail to the wall of the cell, this was not because of its venerable age, but because of its venerable contents.

The babblers of a liberal Bible criticism and of an insipid modernism did not imagine what was possible in the hell of Siberia.

This book has not been written with ink by the spirit of man, but with fire from the spirit of God, and it has been sealed with the Blood of the Son of God.

Hence our God is no silent God! He speaks daily, hourly, to you, through this holy book. Or to put it more concretely, God addresses you and awaits an answer from you.

And now a question of conscience. Every Mohammedan has his Koran and reads it. Every orthodox Jew treasures his Talmud. And should you, a Christian, have no love for Holy Scripture? Does the Bible stand forgotten in your bookcase, where it is dusted off every four weeks?

Possession alone is not enough. You are like the beggar who dies in want, in front of the full treasury, because he has no key to open it. Open this book—open it in reverence, not in a club chair as one would open a Graham Greene or Guareschi, with cigarette in mouth.

Today's best-sellers will pass away; God's word remains for eternity.

God would like to speak to you today, and He awaits your answer.

CHRIST
and the Child-murderess

HOW is it that with learned theological, medical, and social considerations we cannot do away with an evil that threatens to destroy our old Europe?

Perhaps a little story, can, like a stroke of lightning, throw light on the tragedy more concretely and more dramatically than many arguments.

It is told of the infamous king, Herod, that, persecuted by memories and phantoms, he went from place to place, and yet he could not free himself from his feeling of guilt. His sin was that he had murdered all the male children under two years of age in and around Bethlehem.

One day when he was going through the country, he suddenly saw the soul of a child coming out of a house. The king stormed into the house and saw a woman who was permitting the crime of abortion. "Why," he cried at her despairingly, "am I alone persecuted by evil spirits as a murderer? You have done the same thing; you are a murderer, too."

See, dear woman, your doctor has such beautiful excuses as medical diagnosis and similar conscience-soothers, which Satan himself has smuggled into the medical books. But today your conscience should be shocked so that you at least see the evil as an evil when King Herod shouts it into your face.

If that smells too much like the Bible and a Catholic sermon, perhaps you would prefer to hear the Swedish evangelical doctor who, in fright, writes about the crime of abortion. It is not the complaint of a strict pastor, but of a modern doctor. Only an unnatural mother with a frozen conscience can remain unmoved by it.

This man complains about his country, where abortions are very numerous. Some go so far as not to balk at abortion through Caesarian operation in the sixth month.

That means, dear woman—so says the doctor—the child is so far developed that one recognizes the members of the body. (The immortal soul was already there in the first hours of conception. Did you not know that?) And this child lives after removal from the womb for four whole hours. That is two hundred and forty minutes! And then there are still three hours. What are you doing, dear woman, during this time? Or do you wish to help things along with an injection? Then the child still lives two hours, to die slowly like a wounded animal. If anyone would handle an animal in this way, the Society for the Prevention of Cruelty to Animals would call for punishment. But it is only a helpless human with an immortal soul. And then the little thing lives on for another hour before finally dying. And do you believe that the accusation of child-murderess is too strong here?

All this is actual, medical fact.

Even if many have risen up against this statement of the Swedish doctor, or if a whole nation is dreadfully shocked, the facts cannot be denied.

It is good that it was not a pastor who put it in this manner.

And in spite of this, who wishes to throw the first deadly stone at that woman, who often in her confined living quarters has no room for more cradles, who, with wrecked nerves, acted on the spur of the moment, or was mercilessly driven to this act of desperation? Here only God can speak the last word. And, as we hope, a merciful God.

Prayer of an Unborn Child

Father of all life, You have given the right of life to every man. My mother wished to give me life. My father has brought her to this frightful deed. According to man's estimation, I was only eight weeks old. But what does that matter? I already had an immortal soul. My three brothers were permitted to live and may at some time see the face of God. But I complain to my mother that I must go into eternity without having received the sacrament of baptism. Let me not be an avenger of my parents, but an intercessor. Give them the grace to atone for their sin and to be sorry for it.

CHRIST
and Suffering

THE following story may be found in a school primer. One day in the height of his joy—for he was secretly married to a beautiful maiden from Bernau—the proud prince of Bavaria, Albrecht, rode out to the city gate. On the arch of the gate, he discovered the following words written with chalk: "I have cross and suffering, and I write it with chalk. And he who has no cross or suffering, let him erase these lines."

"Go, servant, and erase those lines! For I am happy and without suffering," said Albrecht.

"Your Grace," answered the servant, "you should not do that; no man is without suffering."

He had just begun to carry out the command, when a rider with loose reins sprang through the gate.

"Prince Albrecht, just now your beautiful young wife was drowned in the Danube flood!" he panted.

Albrecht grew pale and said to the servant: "Go and write it again on the arch, and no one shall ever erase it. I have cross and suffering."

A child's story? Yes, but full of deep wisdom and

theology. For suffering belongs inevitably to the life of a Christian.

It is heresy to speak only of a triumphant Church, without at the same time referring to suffering.

It is heresy when modern Christians wish to remove this suffering from the world—whereas it is in the world with a frightful but fruitful reality.

It is a heresy to ignore the suffering in this world by pretending it does not exist, as the joyful world-improvers seek to do.

Christianity will always be a theology of the cross. God the Father has thus willed it, and His Son, Jesus Christ, has affirmed it. The life of Jesus is a proof of it.

Since the existence of original sin, there has been a landslide of cruelty, crime, and sin over the world. Guilty mankind went in a death caravan to hell.

If matters had gone according to the wish of St. Peter, who at that time did not understand that redemption had to be bound up with suffering, this death procession would have had to continue unceasingly to destruction. But Christ stood with outstretched arms before the gates of hell, and through His passion and death He preserved us from it. The chains of sin were thereby broken, and our guilt was expiated.

Suffering has, indeed, remained on this earth after His redemptive act. But it is no longer ill-fated and meaningless. Like a red thread, like a trace of blood from the cross of Christ, there runs through all the letters of St. Paul this thought of suffering that no rationalistic theology can argue away. Even nature itself and creation "yearns and travails in pain until now." (Rom., 8:22)

Noble pagans, without knowledge of Christ, have experienced suffering, and they have tried to explain its mystery. Few indeed in antiquity have borne it in the right spirit. To most, it had to remain an inexplicable fate.

Even the atheist, Nietzsche, knew that no one could get rid of suffering, a fact which he used as a proof of the value of man.

Must we enumerate the many forms of suffering, when daily and hourly we experience the stations of this way of the cross, of misfortune and need, of failure and abandonment, of sickness and death?

To our modern pagans (also to Christians), accustomed to comfort and lack of friction in life, suffering must seem folly, about which they can only shrug their shoulders. Suffering as a friend's service to God is incomprehensible to our effeminate contemporaries. To them the Calvinistic error must be more appealing, namely, that good fortune and prosperity are a special sign of the love of God—provided that it exists for them—although world history, and especially the history of salvation, proves the opposite with a thousand examples.

But that which is foolishness for pagans is for us Christians the voice of God. Christianity recognizes completely the reality of suffering. Christ has trodden the way of the cross and has suffered like any man.

Let us give to ourselves the answer of the good thief on the cross, because a man in the face of death has clearer knowledge. "This one suffers innocently; we, justly." In this we are included, we men of today.

It is always a noble thing for a Christian to see suffering as a just punishment from God for one's faults. But how can one explain the innocent suffering of those persecuted mothers and children, beginning with the murders at Bethlehem and continuing to the starving children of Vietnam!

Unbelievers ask this question sooner than the one who is struck by suffering, for he considers it, though borne with bloody tears, as atonement. We Christians know that innocent suffering is the surest and shortest way to God.

But we admit that much suffering remains a dark mystery that we cannot penetrate with commentaries. Here the words of Christ hold a redeeming and comforting answer for the faithful.

The world says: "We wish to have something from life, and we should like once and for all to forget our cares.

But Christ says: "Blessed are the sorrowful for they shall be comforted."

The world says: "It serves him right when he does not make progress. Why is he so stupid and why does he follow the laws of the Church so closely?"

But Christ says: "He who confesses me before men, I will confess him before my Father who is in Heaven."

The world says: "A person must not show off his Christianity when he knows that under the ruling power it may cost him his life."

But Christ says: "Blessed are those who suffer persecution for justice's sake. For theirs is the kingdom of Heaven."

The world says: "How can one bury himself in a monastery these days when there is so much in life to enjoy?"

But Christ says: "He who wishes to come after me, let him deny himself, take up his cross and follow me. For he who wishes to save his life loses it and he who for my sake loses his life, saves it."

CHRIST
and the Unwed Mother

LORD, men are horrible creatures at times.

There are many Pharisees who allow a mother with an illegitimate child to run the gamut of disgrace. But there are also many liberal contemporaries who plead for the "child of free love." However, that does not change the fact that the sin of the mother remains attached to the child.

It begins with the suffering of being born and reared without the love of a father.

And yet, O Lord, these unmarried mothers are often to be esteemed more highly than those women who have murdered the child in their womb. Their way is mostly a way of the cross. How many of them are in anxiety and despair, and in bitter financial need! How many are forsaken, pushed aside, and seek a solution in suicide!

Is it not our fault when so many, in their despair, prepare a coffin instead of a cradle?

Yes, Lord, we men can be dreadful.

Therefore we have begun a "house of life." We have already placed twenty-four cribs there, where these unwanted girls can prepare for the happiness of motherhood without anxiety and insult.

O Lord, bless these mothers, who are often only children, and bless their children who will feel no fatherly love.

Lead many good men to us who will help us to provide new cradles for these little ones, that the frightful death procession of aborted children can be stopped.

Bless our "house of life."

An Actual Letter From A Child

Dear Father,

I am only twelve years old, and I may not come to your lectures. You have already helped so many. Pray for my father. My mother cannot help crying every night because father has left us and has another wife.

My mother must now work in the factory, and things are not going well with us. I am often sick, and my father has never given me so much as ten cents or an apple. That hurts me. But I am definitely not to blame.

Now I have a request. Please write to my father and tell him that what he is doing is not right. Help us so that he may return to us again.

CHRIST
and the Second of November

"DIE peacefully and without thinking much about it! We shall take care of the rest!"

Mockery? No, only the classic advertising of an undertaker's firm.

What is the "rest" that these business men of piety promptly and efficiently take care of—if they are well paid?

A coffin, corpse-cosmetics so that the relatives may have a pleasant look, black-rimmed cards, a black Chrysler for the last ride. In addition: wreaths; candles; appropriate music in the undertaker's parlor and on the way to the grave; arrangements for an appropriate funeral eulogy.

Once a year, on Memorial Day, the gardener will decorate the grave.

Hence all is taken care of.

But we Catholics know more about the dead. For us, cemeteries are not landscaped gardens, which must give way after fifty years to a new city plan, but they are the resting places of our brothers and sisters, whom God will awaken in eternity. For Him the soul is more essential than the "rest."

The words "poor souls" are not merely a sentimental expression, but correspond to a reality which should never let us rest. These deceased need our prayers. For them the night has come in which they can no longer work.

Whatever is not entirely clean cannot come to God, but must be cleansed in fire, as Holy Scripture says.

Therefore these poor souls need our prayers and our sacrifices! Hence, why have you forgotten them—those who belong to you and are in the cemetery? Why do you not pray for the fallen who have gone down somewhere in the Atlantic, or have been buried in Russia, or in the desert sand? Why don't you think of them? Daughter, you of your aged father; young man, you of your fallen brother, and you, young lady, of the husband with whom you sinned before he left for the front?

If they could only appear to you once in a dream and warn you, or ask you! But they have no messenger but the priest who reminds you again and again of that which is said in the book of the Machabees: "It is a good and wholesome thought to pray for the dead." He recalls this ancient Christian practice to your mind.

Romantic memorial celebrations with brass bands are not enough. Or have our Catholic clubs gone so far that they are satisfied with a silent prayer like the Freemasons? Why should not a Christian mayor, together with the officials of the city, pray an Our Father officially?

Without prayer, your wreaths only smother the dead and your candles burn them.

If your services for the dead remain only an empty community service, at which the non-participating, cold relatives, out of sloth or ignorance, do not pray the Our Father, it is time for us to pack up our Christian tinsel.

Do not forget the dead!

Every day at the Holy Sacrifice our Mother, the Church, remembers the souls of our deceased. So there is a second of November daily at every altar, and the monks add to their table prayers the final request: "And may the souls of the faithful departed through the mercy of God rest in peace!

And we? We should not forget and betray our deceased brothers and sisters. Moreover, we do not know when we ourselves will be "poor souls." It could be tomorrow. And then will the children of our children visit us at the cemetery? Who will pray for us then?

Do you now feel the horrible irony of the undertaker's advertising? These business men of piety have not grasped what an eternity is.

But we should think and act otherwise.

Lord and Master, You have said that the night is coming when no one can work. For our deceased this night has come. But to us living, in Your goodness you have given the means of helping them come to eternal life. Let us always be mindful of this fraternal service. Your holy cross should daily remind us that with Your grace we can open heaven to our deceased brothers and sisters in purgatory.

CHRIST
and His Failure

GENUINE prophets have always allowed themselves to be ostracized. That holds especially for Our Lord Jesus Christ, whose life and word, seen from a purely human point of view, were a failure.

Did he not experience a great failure with His own people? They wanted to stone Him, and for this they took Him outside the city. His relatives rejected Him. What did He leave undone for these people? He satisfied their hunger. He healed their sick. He taught them. He wrought miracles and made great prophecies.

Was that not a failure when the two disciples on the way to Emmaus, with lame wings and flags at half-mast, declared the bankruptcy of their religious expectations, when after three years of effort, He was betrayed and denied by His disciples, and finally had to end His life like a criminal on the Cross?

The lot of Christ is the lot of His Church, which is Christ living on. Therefore, the links of the failure in this His Church are not broken.

Is it not a failure when the world, in spite of the love-message of Christ, after two thousand years still freezes in an ice age of hearts because the gulf-stream of love has been deflected?

Is it not a failure when, from the one teaching of Jesus Christ, a hundred errors have been drawn?

Is it not a failure when the Church that wished to conquer the world is now practically in retreat in Europe?

Is it not a failure when the Church to which victory was promised is constantly outdone by the power of Satan?

Is it not a failure when even popes, the representatives of Christ, have soiled His countenance with their sinful lives, and when fallen-away priests serve as foreign legionaries of Satan?

Is it not a failure when Christians who should bring fire to the world so often sleep behind the stove?

Is it not a failure when even the advance guard of the Church is fearful and suffers from the poison of cowardice?

Is it not a failure when Christians in the morning eat the Sacred Bread at the altar, and in the evening feed on the husks of swine?

As an excuse one might say: "The eastern nations of pagans increase by thirty million while the Christian western land has only a small increase in population."

One might also say that Christianity is not a two-thousand-year inheritance. It must be gained anew by each generation; that is, the father can be a saint and the son a fool. Each one must begin anew.

Moreover, the two thousand years of the existence of the Church, compared with the age of the human race, is a matter of seconds, in which mankind cannot be reformed. The Church is just beginning. Wars and catastrophes have again and again nullified her most valuable gains.

Indeed, these objections would not lead an unbeliever out of the labyrinth. Only the believing man knows how to explain the words of Christ in a divine perspective, and to recognize a victory of Christ and the Church in the apparent failure.

Here considerations of history and psychology must step aside. As true as is the Son of God, so true is His consoling assurance: "Did not the Christ have to suffer these things before entering into his glory?" (Luke, 24:26)

Before His death Christ gave an abundance of references to His own failure. He reached the culmination of His failures on Good Friday, but only Easter morning revealed their true significance. Holy Scripture is full of indications and prophecies: "If they have hated me, they will also hate you."

"The disciple is not above the master"; and also: "Fear not, little flock!"

Are we as stupefied as the disciples at Emmaus that our eyes do not open? It is always Good Friday and Easter morning for the Church.

So the faithful see the failure with other eyes.

Is it not a victory when at all times the Christians,

whether on the martyr's stake or in the diabolic torture chamber of the modern great inquisitors, have remained unshaken witnesses of the truth?

Is it not a victory when the joyful news of Jesus Christ, in spite of Satan's priests and false prophets, has been retained unfalsified, and when not an iota of the teaching of faith has been given up?

Is it not a victory that the Church has outlived enemies like Henry VIII, and Napoleon who imprisoned the pope?

Is it not a victory that mission lands, in spite of the frequent bad example of the West, are in favor of the teaching of the Church?

Is it not a victory that in a greedy and lustful world legions of men and women serve God in strict orders, or have cast themselves into the breach, against unbelief on the most dangerous fronts?

Is it not a victory that thousands of young men, with strength from the Cross, say YES to wasting away and lifelong sickness?

Is it not a victory when, today, Catholics who are so much cursed forgive their persecutors and bless them?

Do you see how the failure of the Church and of Christians, in the end, always turns into victory?

Whenever death bells have tolled for the Church, the Easter bells have always rung more clearly, and have strengthened in us the inevitable belief: "This is the victory that overcomes the world—Our Faith."

CHRIST
and the Red Paradise

WHAT you read in the following lines is not a fable. It was a hundred years ago when the first Communists, with glowing words, promised to workers a social paradise. Bebel announced that through the development of great industry unimaginable results could be attained. The working hours would be cut in half. An Italian communist even spoke of a two to three-hour work day.

In this new, noble state a new kind of man would arise. A kind of superman was prophesied. Platos, Galileos, and Goethes would stand at every street corner, for every worker would now have time to educate himself. There would be no more prisons or barracks. Men in Sunday clothes would run the machines, and even children could relieve their parents. And there would be no hunger and no want.

Of course, the great theorists of the workers' paradise did not picture it so naively. They built it up scientifically. But science and faith in prophecies are so mixed with one another here that it is difficult to separate scientific and religious thought. Thus one can understand that Communism was condemned as a religion rather than as a scientific theory or party.

One who, like Carl Marx in England, had seen the starved figures who, after a sixteen-hour working day, returned to homes in cellars, can understand the passionate protest against such abuses. Often tubercular children of thirteen were employed in the mines. While the workers slept, the rats ate their last piece of bread.

The diagnosis that Carl Marx gave on the ground of such wretched existence was right. But the path that he pointed out for improvement led inevitably to a society without love. With glowing words and prophetic speech, Marx explained to the workers that conditions would get worse for them, but that for the generation of the proletarians there would be a paradise.

With religious and even mystic formulas, the joyful message of a social redeemer was announced. Marx and his disciples sound as if they are prophesying when they theorize about an end-to-misery and speak of their faith in progress.

In this new workers' paradise there would be no sin —by sin is understood the evil of private property.

Machines will play a very decisive role in this wonder-kingdom.

From this scientific foundation, this dreaming Communism, especially in Italy, come illusions about the future, which the little man still repeats in prayer when he paints his social Utopia.

Let us not deceive ourselves. Today's Socialism also, which is the stepchild of Carl Marx, unconsciously marches towards this Utopia.

What answer do we Christians give to this?

We must take the fervor of Communism very seriously. We are not thinking of the amateur communists, who turn to Communism because they are selfish and cowardly. The real communists are fervent. And that is the big advantage which they so often have over us who "know," for "to be fervent" is more than "to know."

We dare not be satisfied with a primitive brand of anti-communism. We Christians know only one brand of anti-communism; that is the one of greater social justice. Otherwise Christ will take more seriously the cry of despair of the communist Marx, than the charitable bandages with which some well-meaning Christians think they can heal the social tragedy.

It is not difficult to refute Marxism scientifically. The prophecy about the end of misery for workers in the Carl Marx sense has by no means been fulfilled, and it must be admitted that for many workers things are going very badly. But wages have doubled since the time of Marx, and the hours of work have been reduced. Moreover, working conditions have been improved. And what about the Marxist belief in progress? We know that big industry is by no means the most favorable solution. On the contrary, we strive for a democratizing of industry, and we wish to do away with the mammoth corporations.

But of what help are all historical arguments? One cannot emphasize enough that "Socialism is not known but believed." That alone is the plane on which Marx can be refuted. It is idle to struggle over peripheral social questions when the promises are not clear. Marxism is based on materialism. It does not believe in an after-life. Here the dividing lines part once and for all. Because it does not believe in God and eternity, it must put its emphasis passionately on an earthly paradise. For every man longs for happiness.

One should not take ill our mistrust of today's moderate Socialism. It is good to know that the English Socialist Party has given up its militant atheism. That does not hold by any means for all countries. And in other states concerned, it is true that leading men are often dissidents and exchange the party book for the Bible.

There is no purpose in letting the paper house of communism cave in, if we have nothing positive to put in its place. Our creeds speak clearly of an eternal God, not of eternal matter. For an educated man it is too stupid not to believe in God. In our creed the word concerning eternal life is very clear. It does not speak of a paradise in this world.

If we take our creed seriously and if we believe in the all-powerful God, we must continue to preach our unpopular teaching of the "valley of tears."

Eternal happiness is not the same as the earthly millenium of fanatical SS men, nor the messianic expectations of the Jewish people, which once painted with glowing colors a social redeemer. The young Carl Marx inherited from his Jewish ancestors this fervent messianic expectation.

We Christians do not believe in any social paradise with which we hypnotize the masses of workers. When is it to come? Carl Marx already expected it in his time. If everything ends with death, of what interest to a worker is a paradise that he does not enjoy in this life?

Eternal happiness implies that the earth remains a valley of tears. That is not an attitude of tired resignation and does not mean that we see this life as a social chaos. But we Christians are modest, realistic politicians of life! Because of original sin, the paradise on earth has definitely been lost. According to the words of Christ, we shall always have the poor with us. No tractor will make work a paradise for the farmer. There will still be thorns and thistles. In the sweat of his brow he will continue to earn his bread. The most modern machinery cannot make us forget this fact.

The sick also will be with us, and in the twenty-first century there will be sanitariums, perhaps more than heretofore.

Only an after-life, a heaven, can bring the longed-for paradise to tortured humanity.

But it is not true that we Christians look only to heaven, forgetting the things of earth. We shall make every effort to do away with social abuses. It is clear to us that we will not turn the despairing away from the foolish idea of a red paradise if we do not prove to them that, as far as possible, we shall satisfy their longing for peace and happiness here on earth. In the midst of miserable living conditions we cannot use theoretical proofs of God's existence. But with all our proofs of God's existence we are worse than the false prophets of the red paradise if we are not ourselves living proof of God, the living, open Bible (they no longer believe the printed Bible), and if we do not treat social outcasts as brothers of Jesus Christ.

Only when we have stooped to help the poorest men on the shadowy side of life will they see that our Christian vale of tears is more pleasant at all times than the much-praised Utopian paradise of the communists.

Lord Jesus Christ, in view of the communistic world propaganda, we should almost like to believe the voice threatening us that Communism will burn up the whole world. But You led Your chosen people through the Red Sea. Lead us, whom you have redeemed with Your Blood, through this red flood. Your Father did not give the grace and the task of renewing the face of the earth to Carl Marx, but to us Christians, insofar as we are in earnest about Your teaching. Give us the grace to be more fervent about Your message than the communists are about theirs. Only then will we be able to hold off the red flood!

CHRIST
and the Rich Church

IT would be casting pearls before swine to try to dispel the prejudice of those who, against their better judgment, refuse to listen to opposing arguments. It is a very old platitude which passes from generation to generation.

It is not as though the Church were immune to the temptations of money! Without doubt mammon has injured our Church more than anything else. But the Church has always been chastised by God when she failed in this matter.

What shall we answer to the statement that the poor Christ did not have whereon to lay His head (our enemies always work with biblical texts) and that He rode on an ass, whereas the pastor rides in a car?

Now Christ at least wore the accustomed garment of one learned in Scripture (in contrast with John the Baptist). He also had a home, where he lived for thirty years. He attended, and did not hesitate to take part in, a marriage feast, at which He was certainly no killjoy. There were no cars then; therefore He used the customary vehicle, the ass.

He who drove the money-changers out of the temple with a whip, prayed in the temple which was decorated with gold and precious stones. He did not demand that the splendid ornaments of the temple be melted down for the numerous poor, cripples, and beggars who lay before the temple doors.

So we do not have plain prayer rooms, but believe that all the beauty the earth offers should be used in the holy service of God, the Creator of these splendors.

Or has God put gold into the womb of the earth only that it might be stored in the fireproof treasury of the rich? The gilded chalice that is destined for use in the greatest mystery has less gold content than a rich woman's heavy ring.

Woe to a people that offers to God churches unworthy of Him, when the smallest insurance building is erected according to the most beautiful design.

When one speaks of the treasures of the Church it is the pious and antique value of the objects that is meant, rather than the actual money value. Would it not be sacrilege if we wished to sell an eighth-century chalice to an antique dealer? The treasures of the Church would be used to decorate the reception rooms of snobbish high society, and the poor would get no share of them.

Why does no one complain that the state should sell its museum pieces and works of art?

Should the pope sell the splendid antique treasures of the Church or even the churches themselves? They do not belong to him, but to the whole Christian people, including the common workers, who from all over the world stream to Rome.

The monk wears a habit made from rough wool. But when he ascends the altar he puts on a beautiful, precious vestment, as is fitting for the service of God. Should we be sad as long as the bridegroom is here? But when the time comes that we must flee into the cellars from the persecutors, we shall with the same reverence (or still more reverently) with a water glass or a jelly glass and a wooden plate, celebrate the Holy Sacrifice, if it must be, in zebra-striped prison garments.

But what about the rich pope with his luxury?

Mohammedans and believing Protestants admire the figure of the Holy Father. But there is a group of Catholics that again and again get this complaint out of moth balls. We have had popes who were swine-herds and slaves. But when they had to receive kings and princes they could not do so in their shirt sleeves. The Jewish high priest entered the holy of holies in rich, embroidered vestments. Do not forget it. The argument that one should give the wealth of the Church to the poor was once brought up in a hypocritical manner in the presence of Christ. At that time it was put forward by the deceiver and traitor, Judas, "who was a thief." The private life of popes, in its simplicity and unpretentiousness, puts to shame many bourgeois circles.

And the fabulous great possessions of the Church?

Indeed, the Church of the middle ages was rich in

foundations and gifts. But in the process of secularization nearly all of this was stolen by the state. Perhaps the best answer here would be to present some sober figures.

The "rich" Church in Germany today has land, distributed for social purposes, that is not one percent of all the land and forest and agricultural holdings divided among twenty-one thousand owners.

We may well wish that we had still more possessions than we had in the middle ages. For from these riches of the Church of the middle ages, the poor and the sick could be fed. Who else would have cared for them when no Red Cross, no guilds, and no welfare organizations existed? Who would have cared for the despairing aged and cripples, for the orphans and feebleminded, who were fed by the dozens at the monastery gates, or were taken care of in asylums?

But capitalism? Was it not hatched by the Church?

If you argue thus, you are standing in the parlor of those communists for whom the Church has become public enemy number one. For the sake of justice it must be said that not every possessor of capital is a capitalist. But unfortunately, it is often so. Their shameful capitalistic type of conduct should more correctly be called mammonism, which Christ also condemned.

The communists and their stupid Christian imitators always complain that the pope excommunicates the poor communists, but never the rich capitalists. But did not Leo XIII speak against "thieving capitalism?" Have you not read the many encyclicals of Pius XI and Pius XII which have again and again expressed an unpopular condemnation of capitalism? Communism formed a comprehensible social teaching. Capitalism is not such a system. It does not form any concrete party, with pass and party book, that one could condemn.

And what about the church taxes, obtained from millions of the faithful?

It is sad when Catholics begin to discuss church taxes. Probably it would be better if the faithful supported the priests directly, for "he who serves the altar should live from the altar." The problem existed at the time of St. Paul, who also found it a burden to earn his bread as a tent-maker. Moreover, the salary of a young assistant, who leaves school when he is about twenty-five, is much less than that of a laborer today.

Where else does the money of the "rich" Church go?

If you wish to see it once in print: In our country (Germany) one hundred and twenty thousand men and women work for a very low wage in an official capacity in the service of charity, that is, of the poor and despairing. For this work, unfortunately, a certain organization is required. The sixty thousand who have honorary offices do not receive a penny from the Church tax for this work.

Do you know what it means when the state gives one pitiful grant to the fifteen hundred hospitals, with a hundred and seventy-three thousand beds, cared for by religious orders, and when one must beg from our

"Christian state" every kindergarten chair? If these houses can function at all, it is only because the much-maligned Catholic Sister often works to exhaustion.

Picture to yourself the procession of many thousands of cripples who receive, at hundreds of institutions of charity, warm soup from your Church tax, and who otherwise would be pushed around in the world. Many thousands with tuberculosis are cared for with these pennies. Two hundred and sixty recreation homes for mothers and children are indeed not enough. But there is not enough money to make it possible for these to be enlarged or rebuilt. How terrible it would be for our children in institutions if there were not almost five thousand orphanages which take the place of the family. In addition, there are innumerable activities in the sphere of public and private welfare, about which a legion of ten thousand speaks—or rather does not speak. For the eternal complainer, who has chanced to meet with a loveless Sister—perhaps because she was overworked—has a bigger mouth than the hundred and twenty thousand helpers, whose work is not published statistically or by way of propaganda, "because the right hand should not know what the left is doing."

So that is the "rich" Church!

It is not a question here of defending those wealthy Christians who are guilty of sins against society that cry out to heaven. We do not need the stern language of the Communist Manifesto to condemn them. The WOE of the Sermon on the Mount in the Gospel according to St. Luke is enough. This WOE fits those great proprietors and wealthy tycoons who seek to leave the Church to take care of their own responsibilities to society. We cannot stand them against the wall like animals. But Christ will thrust them into the sufferings of hell as happened to the rich Dives.

That WOE applies also to many ecclesiastical circles, who do not act from the right motive and who show a lack of proportion; these ecclesiastics beautify the Church only out of childish vanity and rivalry and do not have in mind the greater honor of God; they obtain a new, more beautiful set of chimes before the slums are taken care of. Precisely these ecclesiastics have not fulfilled the social demands of the popes. We do not deny that even in our ranks mammon always was, and is today, a very great temptation.

"It is easier for a camel to pass through the eye of the needle than for a rich man to enter the kingdom of heaven."

This holds also for those Christians of God's church who have sinned in this matter.

CHRIST
and Line 23

OFTEN I had to use Streetcar Line 23. Very often indeed, because I always went that way to the university.

Every day I saw the same faces—no, there were always other new faces that appeared. But there would not be much to tell about this Line 23 if an announcement in a local paper had not startled me. The death of a streetcar conductor was reported there. He died at the age of forty-five, of a lingering lung disease. Besides that, it was noted that he had faithfully performed his duty on the streetcar for twenty-five years, and for twenty-three of those years had served on Line 23.

That upset me. "My" streetcar conductor. Hundreds of times he had called out the station for me. Hundreds of times he had glanced at my pass. I was never more interested in him than in the advertisement on the window. Yes, it is right, he was always pale, and appeared to be suffering. He took pains to show a fatherly friendliness, even at times when the passengers were rude to him. I believe I know today that, though often exhausted, he dragged himself through the crowd, and that he was elsewhere with his thoughts when he said in a routine way: "Is anyone here without a ticket, please?"

And then I learned more about him: that he had a suffering wife at home; that he had five children to feed, and other great worries; that he himself was afflicted with a gnawing sickness, but did not want to show it in case he would be put on pension too soon.

All that I learned afterwards. And since then my interest has increased.

Yes, Lord, why did I never give this man a kind word? A grateful nod? I scarcely said "Good morning." Why did I not ask a sympathetic question? Perhaps I could have helped him in some way. Now I see the death notice before me, and I feel guilty.

But it is too late.

Is it really too late?

I once read somewhere that when two planets meet in space traces are left behind for millions of years. But when two men meet, two men with souls, should they not leave traces? When they meet and look kindly at one another, yes. That should be enough. Or when they greet one another and wish one another well. What kind of cold "good-day" types have we become, who mean nothing to one another? We should and can recognize Christ in every brother, and yet we pass by one another like soulless streetcars. Yes, Lord, I feel guilty towards all of them, all whom I have passed by.

Perhaps I can make up for it.

Before it is too late, I will offer a cup of hot coffee to the old letter carrier, who always climbs up to us on the third floor.

Before it is too late, I will ask our housekeeper about her family.

I will be more friendly with those who come into my office. Perhaps they have already been at five different offices and have been coldly received there at the window. I do not wish to be the last station of disappointment for them.

I shall speak now and then to the old flower-woman who, summer and winter, stands on the corner. Perhaps I will even buy a flower from her to give to another old person, an old man whom no one visits in his solitude.

And I shall greet in a friendly way the newspaper-woman who is a widow and has five children . . . and the bakery boy.

Yes, Lord, I shall do all that again and again for I feel guilty about the streetcar conductor.

Why am I not more like Christ? If I could meet this man once more, I would make everything right. I would be kind and good to him.

But I shall never see him again, this streetcar conductor on Line 23.

CHRIST
and the Young Worker

THE bosses in the iron works had brought to a seething heat, not the metal, but the hearts of the workers. And now things had gone so far that three thousand men were to go out on strike.

The bosses wanted it, and all objections were shouted down. It was no longer the head that ruled here, but the throat. But there was one conscience that would not melt in this boiling pot, the conscience of a young worker who, as an inexperienced employee, was not noticed by the old foxes.

This young man felt that a strike would be wrong. With the passion of a holy fool, he introduced himself, sprang to the speaker's stand, and spoke against the strike. Hundreds of gray-haired men, who had crawled into their Catholic mouse-holes, listened and admitted that this young man was right. But they did not dare to say it aloud.

Perhaps most of the men thought he was right. But the dictatorial ways of the bosses conquered again. They shouted him down and beat him up.

So I met him some hours later in my room.

What difference did it make that the course of events after weeks of cool consideration showed that the young worker had been right? The "crucify him" of the mob had again shouted down the voice of conscience among the masses. But this crowd could not silence his conscience.

He was only a young worker, one of those who had heard the call of the world-famous Abbe Cardijn, who wished to bring Christ into the working world.

The name Cardijn has been known for a long time as far as the Philippines and South Africa.

He saw the problem of the young workers. Every boy and girl who at the age of fourteen leaves the religious atmosphere of school and home, and is caught up on the work system, easily becomes estranged from God after a few weeks.

Yearly, many millions from among the young workers are lost to the Church.

With a fervent heart Cardijn, because of this situation, began his holy experiment in Belgium, and from there he has brought it to the whole world—to lead the young workers of the world to Christ.

We Germans have learned much from this man. I do not forget the hour of our first meeting. It was in his headquarters in Brussels in 1947 (at a time when people still spat at us Germans in Brussels) when he received me, and I heard with a warm heart his earnest encouragement for our German working youth. And I remember the days that Cardijn visited us in the Ruhr region, and in the ruins of our monastery explained his world-wide plans for the working youth.

At that hour, the idea also caught fire in our courageous young worker. With Christ in his heart, he dared, when his conscience demanded it, to point out to the crowd the injustice of their action.

Only one thing is now needed. But this one thing is so often lacking.

There are so many tasks. It is still no small matter to fight against social injustice in industry. It can cost an individual much courage to stand up against the order to work on Sunday.

To gain a rabid communist for Christian social teaching requires, besides one's ideal, an educated missionary zeal.

To visit his home and to stand at the side of a sick and forgotten worker is a task that will hardly be done by the bosses.

Ask the sincere members of these young worker clubs how often they have opened their hearts for this great cause, how often they have received beatings, and how many genuine successes they have scored.

For these young workers, the main business is not only the mission land that they must gain for Christ. They feel responsible also in the midst of their family and of the neighborhood, yes, even in their free time.

For example, in one city, during a big variety show, for which one young worker had the cheapest ticket in the fourth gallery, four thousand men laughed in a cowardly way when the entertainer told a cheap joke about the papacy. The blood rushed to the head of the young worker and he shouted a loud "pfui."

The entertainer became a little uncertain, and made some kind of excuse.

But the four thousand sleeping Christians were ashamed that only one young worker had the courage to protest.

And this young worker will perhaps tomorrow overturn a newspaper stand where sexual cannibals have spread out their devil's wares before children. Or he will perhaps let some white mice loose during a lurid and sexually-exciting movie. Perhaps that is the last self-defense of a young worker who—since the state government sleeps—knows no other way to prevent the fact of Christ from again being disfigured.

That is indeed not the legal or ecclesiastical way; it is wrong and imprudent, and even the chaplain of his youth club will not approve this method. But he has the foolishness of those saints who, in the eyes of their all-too-careful contemporaries, have acted imprudently. Perhaps the young worker said to himself: "Rather come into conflict with the police than with God."

Only a young worker, but Christ needs him in a world which, on its academic stilts, with liberal foresight, avoids pronouncing His name.

He needed him too on the Good Friday in 1950, when a young worker went through the fast train and put in the hand of each passenger a note that read: "In the death hour of Jesus Christ at three o'clock, we young workers will lay down our work today for one minute to think of the death by crucifixion of our Lord. May we ask the passengers of this fast train to think with us during this minute."

And behold, no one excluded himself.

Yes, God needs men, and God needs these young workers.

CHRIST
and the Robot

WHAT is a robot? A man without a soul.

Where is it manufactured? In the factory of the new men.

Who is the founder of this factory? Lenin.

There, men without God are produced. And insofar as a soul is necessary, Lenin is the engineer of this soul. We ought to be frightened, for Lenin is a world danger and has already placed the heel of his boot on one fourth of the earth.

For me the word robot has a diabolic sound, for it awakens the memory of the beasts of commandants who drove us on with this cry to drag iron rails for thirteen hours.

Did the word robot originate then? Does it have—as is said—its origin during the twenties of this century in Czechoslovakia?

No, these robots have a longer history. The climate in which they could succeed was the liberal economic order. A time with real results, but also a time with terrible effects. For the machine became an iron angel. It made gold out of dirt. It ate the raw material, and it also ate the souls of the workers. The worker who, in the beginning, ruled the machines like a king, was more and more overcome by them. And thus arose the robot, the machine-man that was born of a mother. A sad product of the machine age, that influences us in the country as well as in the city.

There is a robot in Russia. One exists also in America. He is found in Germany, and the economic wonder is not his least accomplishment.

In Russia men are beaten with a whip: in the West, we allow ourselves to be driven with a golden whip. But the one whipped is always a slave.

Do you know the Hennecke type, the robot of the East? There are also Hennecke types in the West.

There are robots in white doctor's jackets, just as in servant's coats, and in the robes of jurists. But the robot proves himself most wicked in the factory.

Have we been hopelessly overcome by this evil, or can we still hope for salvation?

The answer cannot come from cold officials, nor from work psychologists, nor industrial psychologists. For the robot is like one possessed. From Holy Scripture we know that Christ healed such a possessed man. Indeed, His warnings to the robot are not a medicine which is as easy to swallow as the opium of the party demagogue who promises an earthly heaven to the masses.

These Marxist promises stand in opposition to the

prophecy of God that in the sweat of our brow we must earn our bread. Such hard work, however, need not make us slaves. Our fathers worked more than eight hours for half the pay that we earn today. In spite of that, they were not held captive in the claws of the robots. They began their work in God's name and knew that it is witchcraft to make gold from dust. They had a patron saint for every trade, who helped to consecrate their work. Cold-hearted officials no longer know that today. They can only rule robots.

Our fathers could not become degraded to robots because they still recognized Sunday as the Lord's day. But where the staggered shift system is introduced the worker is again made a robot, and on Sunday he is called by sirens, not by church bells.

With us Christians not even an undesirable or unproductive occupation can make us robots. The most common and dirtiest work will bring a blessing if it is done with a good intention.

What does the robot care today about God's blessing on his work? He is interested only in profit, in his salary and in enjoyment. After all, a man must have some compensation. So he balances work with indulgence ranging from the TV set to the whiskey bottle.

The machine makes a man a robot, yes, a cheerful robot, who cries for bread and shows. In ancient Rome there were slaves in chains who inwardly were free and noble. Today our modern emancipated workers have put themselves in chains. You may introduce the forty-hour work week; man will still become a robot if he does not know what to do in his free time.

Let us Christians not deceive ourselves. We shall not save the robot with a pious sermon about one's calling. Christ no longer goes into industry. Our Christian workers must, like Christ, heal the possessed. With all the passion with which they fought for the rights of the oppressed, they must seek to break these chains of slavery.

What a noble accomplishment it would be for the workers if they could obtain spiritual emancipation from the claws of materialism. To bring this about would be a real missionary service, because Christ can address only workers with souls, not mechanical men. But a worker who no longer recognizes Christ's joyful message as the Magna Charta, finally falls prey to the class war of the robot officials.

Our Christian leaders of the workmen must be holy interpreters of the Sermon on the Mount, without words of hate, but with no less passion. Only such leaders will conquer the robot in themselves and then snatch the workers out of the claws of the robot. And as true as it is that a robot is one possessed, so is it true that a praying worker can blast the diabolic power that possesses him.

There is deep wisdom in the simple legend of the old fisherman who rowed a young student over the lake. The student discovered on the oars the words "ora et labora." He said to the old man, "Pray and work is a saying which has lost its value. With work alone one gets through life successfully."

The fisherman, who had hands that had labored much, smiled wisely and began to row only with the oar that was marked labora. Of course, the boat moved in circles. The student looked at him questioningly, and the old man said: "So it is in the world when men only work and do not pray; they move around in circles and do not attain their goal."

The decision lies with each of us: Shall I be a praying worker or a cursing robot?

CHRIST
and the First of May

ON May 1, 1955, in Rome, I saw the tragic split of the two camps of world opinion.

Before the mother church of St. John, there were twenty thousand communists—with hard faces, and with paper hats made from their newspaper UNITA, and placed on their heads to shield them from the sun.

In front of St. Peter's Church at the same hour, two hundred thousand Christians were gathered around their high priest in his red vestments. The Christians were from the whole of Italy, whereas the communists were only from Rome.

Among the arriving guests was Archbishop Montini of Milan, the well-known workers' bishop. On his table were piled the red party books of those who had recognized the deceit of Communism and announced their withdrawal from the party.

This fellow cardinal, as a worker called him in a streetcar, did not come in a stylish car like the party leaders of the other assembly.

What an anachronism the May 1st celebration has

become is proved by the following fact. Whereas worn out workers formerly demanded in May 1st slogans, "We wish to loose our chains," today the worker often comes rolling along to the May 1st celebration in a smart uniform and on a fancy motorcycle. We must admit that today there is an entirely new situation.

It is not to be denied that around the world, not least in South America for example, there are still deplorable conditions for the workers, reminding us of the time of Carl Marx. It is also not to be denied that in the economically flourishing Germany the position of a worker who has several children is far from satisfactory. Let us not be deceived. Our social healing that was fought for, not least by the social encyclicals of Pope Leo XIII, is far from perfect. And in spite of this, the exaggerated cult of the laboring class has begun to be unbearable.

The idea of putting an end to the proletariat in the economic system is no longer predominant. The worker's position has for the most part moved up to the position of the middle class.

In what, then, is the meaning of a May 1st announcement? The Holy Father, in his talk on May 1st, did not overlook the economic needs of the socially undeveloped countries. But with all the necessity for economic reform, he wished that the spiritual and religious de-proletarianizing be placed more in the foreground.

The Catholic labor movement in Holland, after its

social-economic success, learned well that the worker with a thick pay envelope can sink lower than the poorest person in the slums.

Thereafter, spiritual deepening became the chief task. Genuine culture is not a privilege limited to the so-called "educated." "Educated" and "studied" are not the same. We have become very distrustful of the many "intelligence factions" and "universities" which show themselves favorable to the devilment of Marxism.

But a never-ending chain of industrial holidays is no nourishment for the soul's emptiness and the spiritual vacuum in which some workers and students so often stand today. Did not May 1st have a noble significance when it was placed under the motto of the religious de-proletarianizing movement.

That was what the Holy Father meant when, through his enlightening words, he consecrated May 1st as a world holiday. One can live, if necessary, without furniture and without a railway schedule, but one cannot live without a soul.

With this understanding, we in the Ruhr district put May 1st into the Church calendar as early as 1946. The miners brought before the altar their lamps, pickaxes, pneumatic drills and saws, and we blessed them.

One need not fear any clerical bogeys because of that. The religious worker is not asked to give up his reasoning faculty in the sacristy, as is often demanded in the party office. A worker who, for himself and for millions of depressed, works for the religious de-prole-

tarianizing movement, will never be driven into the inferno of an absolute state.

That is what May 1st could mean for us—a world-holiday, not with political slogans or rose red or blood red transparencies under the protectorate of Satan, but a Christian world-holiday under the blessing of God. Only a religiously-anchored and a spiritually-schooled worker will grow to genuine maturity and will put the computing official and the machine into the right perspective.

In the economic and social question, he will not fight less for the rights of his fellow worker—perhaps he will fight more—for his fire will not be put out by the class war of a factory office.

Thirty-six million men are born annually. A large number of them go into the ranks of the workers. They will, perhaps, tomorrow determine the fate of Europe and of the whole world. The future will show whether twenty thousand communists will change the world with their hateful class struggle, or whether those workers who are above all thought of gain will fulfill, as a noble task, their goal of spiritual de-proletarianization.

Lord Jesus Christ, Plato and other great pagan philosophers disparaged manual work. But You blessed work by being born into the family of a worker, and there You lived in the service of Your father.

No worker has been led astray by You, but by us Christians who have so often forgotten our brother in need. Let the workers of the world attain the economic

goods which are the presupposition of a genuine Christian life. Let them not choke in the mammon of this earth, but show them how, above all the cares of this world, they should not forget one task: to know You and Your Father in heaven and to direct their life and work to eternity.

CHRIST
and Check Number 1380-06

"ACCURSED money has hurt the Church more than anything else." This statement is unfortunately all too true. But money is not always the devil's dung. In the kingdom of God it can also be a power for saving souls. For one cannot get rid of hunger and need by disputation, but one must attack them with goods and money.

A check number is sober and cold. (Satan also had his check number.) But with it one can establish a miracle center, through which starved, despairing, broken men can again learn to believe.

The statement that "Christ appeared to the men in bread" cannot be rejected as heresy.

So we have bound ourselves with a check number. We know that such a number has unpleasant associations. But in the twentieth century—since we no longer have bartering—a check is necessary in order to help quickly and efficiently. And if you are still mistrustful, read what this wonder number has already accomplished.

Rent for our brothers—we were able for six months to pay more than ten thousand poor men ten marks a month as a help in paying their rent.

Help for theological students—we were able to help four hundred theologians and students to finance their education.

S. O. S. packages—we were able in the last five years to get food for more than 120,000 persons in the East and West, who were in great need.

Clothing—we were able to beg almost a thousand cubic meters of good clothing and shoes, that is, about one hundred and fifty truck-loads, and thus help thousands of men.

Golden children's village—we were able to build small family orphan homes where good women take the place of mothers—one for each nine children.

Lepers—we were able to furnish the money for a small leper colony in order that these poor creatures might be helped in time.

Recreation home—the poor and sick can rest with us at no cost in a beautiful house in the mountains.

House of life—we were able to begin the construction of a building in which there are already twenty-four cribs to keep unmarried mothers from being guilty of abortion in their despair.

Pagan children—we were able to lead five thousand three hundred pagan children to baptism and instruction in the missions.

Prisoners—we were able to help forty-eight prisoners with books and other articles, and find sponsors to help them.

Sick—we were able to help more than two thousand seriously sick persons by providing sponsors, letters, and gifts.

Behold, on us modern men anxiety lies like a phantom. It is anxiety in view of the last judgment. But why this anxiety? You have eternity in your hand. Christ will ask you personally at the last judgment about the corporal and spiritual works of mercy. And then the judgment will follow with the words: "What you did to the least of my brethren you have done to me." And "What you have not done to the least of my brethren you have not done to me."

Always remember: There is one still poorer than yourself—that is Christ, your Brother.